PUSH!

How to Transform Your Life,
Your Family, and Your Business

Brett Stalcup

Carpenter's Son Publishing

Push!: How to Transform Your Life, Your Family, and Your Business

© 2014 Brett Stalcup

All rights reserved. No part of this book may be reproduced or transmitted in any form or by any means, electronic or mechanical, including photocopying, recording, or by any information storage and retrieval system, without permission in writing from the copyright owner.

Published by Carpenter's Son Publishing, Franklin, Tennessee

Published in association with Larry Carpenter of Christian Book Services, LLC
www.christianbookservices.com

All scripture quotations, unless otherwise indicated, are taken from the Holy Bible, New International Version®, NIV®. Copyright ©1973, 1978, 1984, 2011 by Biblica, Inc.™ Used by permission of Zondervan. All rights reserved worldwide. The "NIV" and "New International Version" are trademarks registered in the United States Patent and Trademark Office by Biblica, Inc.™

Editing by Tammy Kling

Cover Design by Abraham Osuna

Interior Design by Suzanne Lawing

Printed in the United States of America

978-1-940262-23-9

To learn more about Brett Stalcup and PUSH!, visit his websites at
www.StalcupLaw.com and www.PushProgram.com.

Contents

Don't be afraid of problems: learn to PUSH!
through them—PUSH! for togetherness.
PUSH! for communication.

—BRETT STALCUP

Dedicated to Charlie, my brother; to my wonderful wife, Sanka; and to our two beautiful girls. Life wouldn't be the same without you. Also, I want to thank James Morris for his countless hours and honest feedback that he provided. This book has influenced all of us in a positive manner through laughter and hard work.

FOREWORD

Throughout my life I have coached high achievers all over the world, including the CEOs of companies like Walmart, Samsung, and Firestone. I've worked with entrepreneurs to help them achieve better results.

When I first met Brett Stalcup, it was easy to see he was a respected attorney in Dallas who helps his clients recover. But I've learned over the years that it's not just about representing their legal case, but the restoration of lives and families, that matters to Brett.

I coach people through the process of clarity, focus, and execution.

Brett's book *PUSH!* will help you think through and possibly uncover patterns in life and habits that simply aren't serving you anymore. Uncover your blind spots. When I coach people through strategic acceleration, I talk a lot about blind spots. Blind spots are a hazard—just like when you're driving in your car. It's a seemingly invisible thing that can result in disaster and wreckage. If you take action and try to change lanes but you have a blind spot, it could cause an accident and result in a loss of life. And when you do uncover them, Brett says, PUSH! Push through GAF, which is guilt, anger, and fear. Push through insecurities and obstacles.

Do you have old thought patterns that hold you back? Addictions? Unhealthy habits? Or maybe you're very successful and you want to become even more successful and healthy than you already are. We all need to PUSH!

Brett can show you how.

—TONY JEARY
Coach to the World's Top CEOs

INTRODUCTION

Every life has ups and downs. Chances are you've had extremely exciting and joyful moments, such as the birth of a child or a home run in business, and yet low moments too, like a death in the family or that a family member or spouse is struggling with addiction. For some, the loss of a job or money is devastating.

Life is a series of peaks and valleys, but sometimes the valleys are so deep it seems like you won't ever recover. But you will. What we all chase is the area between the peaks and valleys that I call "balance," which is what we all desire to achieve. It's elusive, and no matter who you are, you want more of it because it's in that space where peace exists. Life seems content, slower, and more manageable.

Where are you?

If you're a high achiever trying to juggle realities of life, a job, and a family, it's possible you often feel unbalanced as you strive for more and more, and struggle to make it all happen. Then there are the times we find ourselves in a place where we are facing an unexpected obstacle. The Bible teaches we are either headed into or out of a storm.

Perhaps you relate to the struggle, or the strength part of this message. It's likely you have experienced both. Only you can determine where you are now—in relation to where you want to be. What's that gap look like? Is it a long road to peace, success, and self-improvement? Are you honest enough with yourself to identify your blind spots and get clear about the steps you need to take?

I wrote this book to help guide you along your journey and to let you know that you're not alone.

High achievers (HAs) throughout history have been the most unbalanced people that you could imagine. Thomas Jefferson was a brilliant politician who tried to steal his best friend's wife. Benjamin Franklin was a famous inventor but not a faithful husband. Steve Jobs was a brilliant, successful businessman who had issues with the way he treated people. These HAs left a brilliant mark in history, but they did not live balanced lives.

Please understand that I am not knocking success. These successful men left a beautiful mark on history and they did it their way. But there's a better way, and it leads to a fulfilling existence where your faith, your family, and your work life collide and intersect in a beautiful kaleidoscope of success.

When you strive for hitting a home run in life, while living and representing a mature God-centric worldview, you'll feel much more content and balanced, but you'll also be able to give back more. My mission in this book is to teach you to PUSH! through your obstacles, and see them as opportunities, and to manage life's challenges without losing yourself or your integrity.

We all have struggles. We have all suffered loss. Each one of us has faced a challenge of some sort. In many cases, the challenges became too hard to overcome and resulted in broken dreams. A lot of the clients I see who have gotten themselves into legal battles have in some way given up on their dreams. Perhaps it was the loss of a relationship or loved one, or childhood abuse or other behavior that led to addiction, crime, or poor choices.

I've seen a lot in my years as an attorney representing a variety of clients with various troubles, including addictions that led them to my office seeking new direction. But what if they had recalibrated their life early on and lived according to a set of values and standards that saved them first?

One of my goals in writing this book is to teach you how to think differently and provide you with the tools to manage your life better. It's that simple.

Many clients have gotten so trapped in their own drama and emotion that it's been a downward spiral of reactivity, crime, poor choices, and challenges that have caused them to dig a deeper hole for themselves. But there's a different way. I've learned many of these strategies and coping skills throughout my decades defending individuals, understanding their motives and responses, and listening to their stories. It's my job to help, protect, defend, and strategize. I empathize with my clients and feel a deep personal tie to them because, more often than not, there's been a tragedy in their lives that has led them down the path of bad decisions. Naturally, I want to now share those same strategies for success—the ones I share with them when they're sitting across my desk—with you.

One of my own greatest life challenges was the day my brother Charlie died of melanoma cancer. It changed me. There's no other way to say it. Prior to that moment, I considered death a scary and untouchable thing. Charlie showed me how to live and how to die. It was a tortuous, challenging time in my journey through life.

Imagine watching the person you love struggle with pain, ongoing chemotherapy treatments, numerous surgeries, prescription pills, and the continuous uncertainty of death. It could have shattered me. I could have gotten angry with God and questioned why my brother was taken so young or had to undergo such a torturous disease. My whole family could have played the victim card.

A lot of people do become angry at God when tragedy comes; they even play the victim card. What I have experienced and would like to share is that attitude is everything. The attitude of the person fighting tragedy and attitudes of those around him or her are what create the defining moments.

My brother's cancer started in his back and ended up in his brain. During the three to four years of torture, his attitude was unbelievably positive. He lived with hope and passion. He was never angry or resentful. Charlie lived as if every day was a gift. He told me that "I'm glad it is me, and not you." All along the way, he was hopeful that he'd be cured. He never lived as a victim, and most importantly, he never quit.

He loved being a high school football coach. He could have chosen a more lucrative career, but teaching football to young men was his ministry. The town of Southlake, Texas returned their gratitude by supporting him emotionally and financially. They were there for him.

My brother lived for kids, not money. He was one courageous, smart football coach. My favorite example of his courage was when a group of doctors told him in his hospital room that his cancer was terminal and there was nothing they could do for him. He was going to die. It was so sad. I was crying, and my brother looked me in the eye and said:

"Why are you crying?"

I told him "Because they said you are going to die."

He told me to "Put your shovel down."

"What?" I replied.

"Put your shovel down and hand me my cane," he said, "because I want you to help me walk to the nurse's station. They'll see I am not a quitter and they won't give up on me if I won't give up on them." I was amazed at his strength and courage. I gave him the cane and we made the walk together, arms around each other. He was in severe pain but didn't quit. There was not a dry eye on the entire hospital floor. It was a true lesson in courage.

As I mentioned earlier, Charlie was not rich in money, but he was rich in courage. He wasn't the ultimate high achiever, but he loved his family and fellow man. He loved the kids he coached and the coaches he worked with and cared about them deeply. He lived a mature, balanced life. He trusted God with the outcome and was at peace with dying, but he never quit. After he died, for the first time in my life, I was loss for words. I didn't know what I would say at his funeral. How could I put his journey into words that would honor his life as he deserved?

Preparing for his eulogy was the most difficult preparations I endured. Why? Because "little brother" used to poke at "big brother" for not making enough money; I was sure he was capable of making more.

He showed me!

There were three thousand people at his funeral, and most of them were kids he had influenced. It was amazing to see the love and respect a community had for big brother. Now, I had the opportunity to honor his accomplishments. I started thinking how a number of them kept telling me how they were sorry Charlie lost his battle with cancer. I didn't think that he did. To me that sounds like the makings of a good trial. So I decided to present the case of COACH STALCUP vs. CANCER.

I chose God to be the judge, the attendees were the jurors, and baby brother was the self-chosen lawyer. I started by saying:

DEAR GOD, I CALL MY FIRST WITNESS—THE COMMUNITY.

You can tell a lot about a man and his character by the way his friends step up in a time of crisis.

You can tell a lot about the community by the way it responds to a man's crisis. Charlie had a lot of friends.

The response to his crisis was the type that renewed your

faith in the community. Kids and adults alike pitched in.

Most importantly, prayer was at the top of the list. Everyone would say, "Are you praying for Charlie?"

DEAR GOD, I CALL MY SECOND WITNESS—HIS FAMILY.

Cindy, Cara, Jamie, and Price were there for Charlie. They did not quit on him. Their love and care was persistent. They only wanted the best for their father and husband.

All the other family members were there—mom, dad, Barbara, sister, and little brother. There were no quitters. All had a common goal.

DEAR GOD, I CALL MY THIRD WITNESS—CHARLIE STALCUP.

Cancer might have won the battle over the body, but it never got his spirit. NEVER! He was NEVER a victim. He was a walking testimony with his FAITH. He had the gift of quiet strength. His competitive spirit kept him going. All you had to do was dare him.

His fight was that of a true CHAMPION—passionate, focused, persistent, courageous, and always putting GOD first.

YOU ARE THE JURY—it's your vote. Charlie loved the book *Purpose Driven Life* by Dr. Rick Warren. Charlie knew his purpose. He was living for GOD.

YOUR VERDICT FOR CHARLIE WILL RING LOUD AND CLEAR if we remember it's about God, not about us.

YOUR VERDICT FOR CHARLIE WILL RING LOUD AND CLEAR if we transform this painful experience into our biggest asset for GOD. We can't waste our hurt.

YOUR VERDICT FOR CHARLIE WILL RING LOUD AND CLEAR if we always keep our hope and faith.

During the funeral procession, people lined up on the side of the road; men tipped their hats in honor of my brother.

He was Charlie. What else can I say?

Are you a "Charlie"? Are you living life with passion? Are you hopeful? Are you chasing your dreams? Do you have a ministry? Maybe you're reading this book because you are at that point where the rubber meets the road, and it's time to intervene in someone else's life. Maybe it's your child's. And maybe, it's even your own.

No matter what you've faced in life or what's on the road ahead, it's my hope that this book can offer you inspiration, tools, wisdom, and guidance and inspire you to PUSH! through your problems. Never, ever give up.

You cannot heal or change what you do not . . .

ACKNOWLEDGE.

CHAPTER 1

PUSH!

Look at any individual who has achieved a great measure of success and you'll find they had to PUSH! to make things happen. PUSH! is the unique character trait that enables people to PUSH! through obstacles, temptations, and self-defeating thoughts. Successful people PUSH! when they got tired or defeated, and PUSH! when others said they couldn't do it. Every morning they wake up and PUSH!

Winners and champions aren't quitters. You can't wake up every morning and PUSH! unless you are persistent and committed to your life!

No matter what, winners PUSH! If someone tells them they can't do something, they get up a little earlier the next morning, and they do it. You know exactly the type of people I'm talking about. They are intoxicating. They have drive. They may not be as smart as the next person, or they might be smarter, but one thing you can bet on is that they are going to wake up the next morning and tackle life by the tail. No one tells them it can't be done.

Look at your own life.

Who in your life is filled with positive energy, dreams, passion, commitment, vision, clarity, focus, and faith? Surround yourself with these people. These are the people who are leaders filled with positive energy, and they will assist you in being successful. One individual in my world who has been an inspiration to me is Omar Avilla, the ultimate example of PUSH! Omar joined the army after 9/11 when he saw the towers destroyed. Duty called, and he made the choice to serve his country. He earned the rank of E-5 sergeant, where he conducted numerous patrols in Iraq as a machine gunner on a three-ton Humvee. On May 14, 2007, as he and his five-member team were patrolling, their vehicle ran over a 200-pound deep-buried IED, and it hit the right side of the vehicle.

Omar was a gunner. His vehicle was launched into the air and his legs gave in and crumbled up, broken. As Omar was lying flat in the vehicle, he began making peace with God, unsure if he'd survive. At this defining moment, he decided not to quit but to PUSH! He literally began saving his team while his body was on fire. As he was pulling bodies out of the burning vehicle, he observed his skin melting to the bone. It did not stop him!

Today Omar explains his ability to PUSH! through struggles as an inner light. He raised himself up and jumped to the side as thirty to forty insurgents ran in his direction. As he was on fire, several of his fellow warriors saved him by putting out the flames with a fire extinguisher. His driver began to panic, and Omar slapped him to get his attention even as his own body was still smoking from the fire. Omar made sure his team was evacuated first, and he made numerous choices to push through the worst horror imaginable. Today he's a 27-year-old inspiration, and a warrior who survived the attack.

No one sprinkled Omar with magic dust to keep him pushing that day. He was the magic dust. Nick Vujicic, an Australian motivational speaker with no arms or legs, often says, "If you can't get a miracle, be one." This is the philosophy I am bringing to you today, right here, right now.

You are the one who is going to change the direction of your life.

You are the one who is going to replace the negative tapes that stifle you with positive, successful tapes that create you. You are going to wake every morning and say: I can.

You are going to PUSH! through any obstacle, barrier, addiction, or curveball thrown at you. And not only that—but you'll change lives in the process. Your goal should not just be to change your own life, but to be a world-changer who positively impacts the lives of others.

You are a newly claimed winner and champion just like Charlie—just like Omar.

The most important quality you can possess in life is persistence (the ongoing ability to PUSH!). Over the years I've learned that sometimes the one who wins is the one who shows up the most. Persistence is about being aggressive with your goals and dreams, versus passively waiting for them to come true. Persistence means that when you hit a roadblock, you keep going and find another way around. Persistent people win more often than passive people because they find ways to get things done.

Persistence can also be explained by examining faith and hope. Think about it! God creates persistence by having us rely on faith for answering prayers. I am not a preacher, but I have witnessed the miracle through my clients many times. It is amazing to watch an addict who is new to recovery find God and let Him into his heart. I have witnessed God answer prayers quickly to show them they made the right decision to come to Him. It builds their faith to receive this quick response to prayer.

Sometimes I wonder why the more seasoned, disciplined believer has to wait years to see an answer to his or her prayers. Is it because God is teaching us patience? Is it to teach us to be faithful and persistent? Is it to teach us how to pray until something happens? Only God knows.

Winners are persistent.

They don't quit. They keep on until they are finished. They will not give up even when the hardest obstacles imaginable are facing them. They figure out a way to win: they have big dreams, yet they always figure out the right thing to do.

What are your dreams?

My goal in writing this book is to help fuel you to dream big. I can't help you go through the motions to achieving your dreams—no one can. But I can encourage you to think like a champion and dream big.

What is it you want to do? Anything is possible.

You may have had an idea brewing in your heart for years, but it is one thing to think of ideas. It is another thing to finish ideas. I hate it when someone says, "Oh, I wish I had thought of that idea." My response is, "Do it and do it from beginning to end!" Not everything takes money. There are plenty of entrepreneurs who have been successful with little or no seed money. They use their talent and gifts to succeed. The common element is they don't quit. You've got to have persistence, but you can't be negative about your ideas. Have confidence! Winners have faith. They trust and lean on God for answers. They pray for God's will. They know without God in the deal, it might be successful, but it will fail without Him in it. I can think of the times when I wanted things in my life no matter what. I did whatever it took to pull the trigger. As I look back to each of those times, I can tell you when I was in it and God wasn't.

The difficult challenge in relying on faith is that it requires patience. I want answers now! He wants you to learn. He wants you to wait. God has wisdom. I have the ability to grind myself into a decision. Yet those decisions are usually bad ones. Maybe we should allow God to dictate the course instead of intellectualizing everything. It may take more time, but it's a smarter and clearer way to get to your destination. With God's oversight, you are going to live the powerful, joy-filled life that you deserve.

This is the second part of the title, which focuses on you praying until something happens. It's one thing to get excited and make a choice to PUSH! every morning. It is another to pray to God to direct you in the path He wants you to go. It is difficult to allow Him to deliver His will and not yours. It is difficult to allow Him to fill your heart with passion. God will give you what he wants you to have: a joy-filled, peaceful, loving, and passionate life.

What's your dream?

EXERCISE

Make a list of your dreams, and don't place any fences around them. If you could have anything, what would it be? If you could go anywhere, where would you go? If you could meet anyone, who would it be? Make a list of your dreams, even if they're old, dead and buried, or seem out of reach. Once you put dreams on paper, it will be easier to see which ones are dreams you need to revive and which ones are just fantasies.

_____

_____

_____

_____

_____

_____

_____

_____

_____

_____

_____

_____

_____

CHAPTER 2

Freedom

Many of the people I've worked with throughout the years have arrived at a place of destruction or poor choices because they're in bondage. Freedom is the opposite of being tied up and bound to something. Bondage is a result of a stronghold such as addiction to one thing or another, whether it's a drug, alcohol, some other substance, or a series of unhealthy relationships or emotional outbursts. Bondage creates a domino effect of tragedy, family problems, divorce, breakage, and destruction.

No matter who you are and how successful you may be, you need to be free. Freedom is the ultimate currency. I've seen financially successful CEOs in bondage and I've seen poor people in bondage, and they're always the same. They are nervous, anxious, fearful, angry, or limited because they're tied up in their own mind. Bondage usually doesn't happen overnight. It's the result of a pattern of unhealthy actions, habits, or thought processes, and usually all three combined.

The road to freedom and living a balanced life is often written as a complex scientific psychological phenomenon, but it's not complex at all. My experience as a trial lawyer, motivational speaker, and mentor has led me to the truth that living a simple, successful life creates peace.

I have discovered that if most kids are given a simple formula to follow, along with mentorship, that they can live as winners in life and not losers. As adults, we can follow this formula as well.

A lot of the younger clients I see who have gotten themselves into legal trouble have in some way given up on their dreams. The parent might think it is just addiction we've got to take care of, but it is usually much deeper than that. Addiction has roots in people's hearts, and most of the time the reliance on drugs or alcohol is an escape—a way to mediate pain. Their pain may originate internally or externally.

Perhaps it was the loss of a relationship or a parent, or being the victim of childhood abuse or divorce, that led to addiction, crime, and poor choices. In many cases, the challenges became too hard at an early age to overcome and resulted in broken dreams.

Families with trauma are seeking answers, not scientific principles. Parents call me and say, "Brett, my kid's on heroin; I need help." They don't call and say, "Brett, my kid's on heroin; he needs off." My response is, "Bring them in; they deserve freedom."

I have learned through the years, after obtaining feedback from my clients, that they want immediate answers. They don't want to have to run to the library and research a lengthy, scientific novel to discover the answers. They are in a panic. I've had so many parents sit across from my desk that I learned to distill the formula into three simple words for their family to live by: BALANCE, BELIEVE, and BE.

Balance

As parents, we should all seek to obtain BALANCE in our kids' lives by learning how to obtain freedom, manage our feelings, and make mature decisions. Sometimes just being there for them is the answer.

As I tell my clients, you can spend time with your kids now or later on, when they are in drug rehab or a treatment program.

Believe

Parents need to also teach their kids how to BELIEVE in themselves again and learn to not only trust our judgment but to trust God. They have to learn how to say no to peer pressure, and it's a parent's job to teach that, not preach that, but teach it over and over and over again.

This formula applies to you whether you have kids or not. It applies to each one of us.

Be

Each one of us has to learn to BE ourselves, that one individual human whom God created us to be. He created us to walk our own path, not someone else's. He teaches us to be ourselves and to teach our kids to be themselves. We have to nurture their traits, even if they are much different than ours. We have to help them grow.

My life has not been perfect. In my youth, through my adult years, I had seasons of challenge, growth, and freedom. It is the sum of all those experiences and my will to PUSH! every day—not just my strengths but the challenges, too—that allow me to relate to my clients and families when they are at war. When I see families sitting across the conference table in front of me, struggling with life, addiction, or any other criminal law issue, I seek to help them resolve the core issue causing the pain or addiction so they will never have to come back. Other lawyers think I am crazy when I teach that philosophy, but a healed family with positive results sends a better message to the community than repeat offenders.

Computers, Xbox, and cell phones do not teach kids these principles, parents do. Jeremiah 1:5: "Before I formed you in the womb I knew you, before you were born I set you apart; I appointed you as a prophet to the nations." That verse doesn't say that God knew you, but that He set you apart. You are a winner and a champion! And you were one before you were born. Kids get lost when they live in the cave of technology. We need to pull them out and teach them to communicate (talk). It is imperative that you go back to the basics and teach them the difference between right and wrong. The kids of the current generation desire to be led. Unfortunately, we have spoiled them with money instead of teaching them to work.

This book is not only about changing families' lives but also to encourage you to help other families obtain the tools to live a balanced life. It will give you the tools to help other families to learn to trust again and to move toward their goals and dreams along the way. You might be the one person who helps a kid "out of the ditch" by helping them through the addiction. Don't you agree that kids deserve a fresh start? I personally feel each one of us does.

People say life's a journey, but I believe it's more about conquering the challenges that face you than just "living the dream." If we can teach families to grow, give, love, and serve by living a more balanced life and believing in themselves, we will reach the potential and destiny that God has for our kids' lives.

EXERCISE

Open your mind and make a prayer list.

_____

_____

_____

_____

_____

_____

_____

_____

_____

_____

_____

_____

_____

_____

_____

_____

EXERCISE

What is it you need to be free from?

_____

_____

_____

_____

_____

_____

_____

_____

_____

_____

_____

_____

_____

_____

_____

_____

_____

_____

CHAPTER 3

Addiction

This book wouldn't be complete if I didn't talk about addiction, because it has been my experience that most people are addicted to something. It might be shopping, eating, drinking, Facebook, or a substance addiction, but often it's too late and marriages have ended before the addiction is uncovered. When people get into legal trouble from their addictions, it can lead to many more issues, such as jail time, money spent on criminal defense, family breakdown, health issues, stress, and emotional suffering.

Addiction often has its roots in something else. When people come into my office and have an addiction issue that has stimulated criminal activity, often there's a root pain.

Maybe it's abuse or their parents' divorce. It could also be a disappointment, abandonment, or a childhood wound. In those cases it's important to find the root of pain and start weeding. Addiction has to be conquered before an addict or his family can recover.

Sometimes addiction is the result of physical or emotional abuse. It's a pain in the heart that just never healed. In those situations, you have got to heal the pain or the cycle of addiction just continues. Many addicts quit one addiction and continue on to become addicted to something else, such as sex, pornography, drugs, alcohol, food, or spending too much money. An alcoholic might get free of alcohol and then get addicted to something else. A love addict might get addicted to sex, or a former sex addict may turn to excessive shopping or food.

If you've ever seen the television show *Hoarders* you can see how the individual profiled has a life of chaos that often extends far beyond the hoarding. The person is often either obese or disheveled and unkempt. It's not just the hoarding of items or shopping that is the addiction. They're doing it to cover a gaping hole that only God can fill. It is a void in the soul and a pain in the heart.

Sometimes a child or teen gets exposed to a drug, and an addiction forms on its own. The addiction *is* the addiction. Maybe they've got great parents but can't lose the drug. Their body becomes chemically dependent. In those cases, the individual has to be removed from the addiction and has to make a commitment to recovery. Also, the parents should not feel guilty and drive themselves crazy by researching the family chain for alcoholism or drug addiction. It is not about the parent as much as it is about the addiction.

It is important for people to know the difference between "use," "abuse," and "addiction" when working with substance abuse. "Use" consists of the appropriate consumption of alcohol or a drug. It means the proper user is taking the prescribed drug or alcohol. The next level is "abuse." When minors use alcohol, it is considered abuse. When someone consumes a prescription that was prescribed for someone else, it is considered abuse.

Abuse also involves continued consumption of alcohol or drugs despite adverse consequences. A person who drinks too much or too often could still be abusing alcohol, rather than being considered alcohol-dependent or alcoholic. This could be the weekend warrior or a person who misses work on more than one occasion because of getting drunk.

"Addiction" is when a person becomes physically and psychologically dependent on drugs or alcohol. An alcoholic drinks for long periods (it takes more alcohol to get him drunk over the longer periods), becomes tolerant to the effects of alcohol, drinks at work, has withdrawal symptoms when he doesn't drink, has cravings, and misses social and family activities because of his dependence on alcohol.

The cause of alcoholism is not well established, and there's controversy over how to treat it. This is a major problem with treatment, as many people, psychologists, and treatment experts will prey on alcoholics by trying to sell the next quick fix to alcoholism. For example: Take this pill and you are fixed. Take this shot and you are fixed. Take this intravenous drip and it will repair the damage you have done to your brain due to alcohol.

There is growing evidence for genetic and biological predispositions for this disease, but the research is controversial. Children of alcoholic biological parents have increased risk of becoming alcoholics. Research has implicated a gene (D2, the dopamine receptor gene) that when inherited in a specific form might increase chances of becoming an alcoholic. Twice as many men are alcoholics. The simple fact remains that if you shoot or snort heroin, you can become addicted after one time.

Alcohol addiction occurs gradually as drinking alters the balance of chemicals in your brain, such as gamma-aminobutyric acid (GABA), which inhibits compulsiveness, and glutamate, which excites the nervous system. Alcohol also raises the levels of dopamine in the brain, which is associated with the pleasurable aspects of drinking alcohol. Excessive long-term drinking can deplete or increase the levels of these chemicals, causing the body to crave alcohol to restore good feelings or to avoid negative feelings.

Other factors can lead to excessive drinking that contributes to the addiction process. These include:

Genetics. Certain genetic factors may cause a person to be vulnerable to alcoholism. If you have an imbalance of brain chemicals, you may be predisposed to alcoholism. In the recovery world, we use the term "you have the gene" when a person has the family history. The point being, your family has a history of alcoholism, so why don't you stop the chain with you?

Emotional state. High levels of stress, anxiety, and emotional pain can lead some people to abuse alcohol. The alcohol is used as a method to medicate this hurt.

Psychological factors. Having low self-esteem or suffering from depression may make it easy for you to abuse alcohol. Bipolar and ADHD patients will medicate with alcohol and drugs instead of prescription drugs. They choose to drink alcohol rather than admit they're bipolar and properly manage their psychological state.

Social and cultural factors. If you hang with people who drink a lot, you are probably going to drink a lot. That is, alcoholism can become a learned behavior. This is why Alcoholics Anonymous teaches you to change people, places, and things when trying to get sober. I mention all of these things because in my work as an attorney, I've seen accomplished professionals struggle with things like alcoholism and then get free from it. Once they are free, they are free to achieve their dreams. They have clarity.

In my career as an attorney, I have had the opportunity to work with people in all phases of life. Some are going through bad times, and there does not seem to be a light at the end of the tunnel. A lot of the time, though, people are going through things they have created for themselves. Relationship conflict, career struggles, or trouble with the law because of negative decisions they've made along the way. But one thing I have seen in every situation is that people deserve a second chance.

If you are a champion, you have to persevere—PUSH! That is, you do not quit. You keep on fighting for freedom. It does not matter what addiction you are faced with; chances are there is someone you know who has dealt with it before.

There are different levels of drug, sex, and alcohol addiction treatment. First and foremost, Alcohol Anonymous should be included in any recovery/treatment program. Level one is drug/alcohol counseling. Level two would include outpatient treatment. Level three would include inpatient treatment from thirty days to one year, depending on the diagnosis and severity of the addiction or whether the addict is a repeat offender.

Aftercare programs should be included after inpatient treatment to continue the recovery process. Today, we are finding that longer treatment is necessary to beat addiction because the drugs are so extreme and tough to kick. Sober living houses are a wonderful addition to aftercare programs as they assist the client working themselves back as a working member of society. If you or a loved one make a mistake and then make a decision to turn in the other direction, there is an opportunity to erase and rewrite the past. Recovery and restoration are both possible in every situation.

Other monitoring programs are available at various levels to help a person stay free of alcohol. They are more or less a paid accountability program—and they work. They provide random urinary analysis, sponsor reviews, family interviews, written reports from recovery, and follow-up with counselors.

It all starts with believing. You've got to believe that it can be done. Doubt and fear will result in a relapse. I don't care what anyone or institution attempts to sell, faith has to be a major ingredient in the recovery process. How can someone seek freedom from bondage without faith and guidance from God? It will not happen. It is too big a burden and fight to take on without faith.

Addicts and alcoholics who are committed to a recovery

program have the best chance for success. They believe in it. They trust it. For the first time, they are in a position to listen and learn as they are committed to the program. The key is that they have made that decision. Sometimes people get so tired of failing and the wreckage that the failure creates that they are determined to make a different choice; other times they are forced into it by a legal situation, an encounter with the law, or some other tragic event. Commitment to restoration is the key. To beat addiction, each person or family member affected has to wake up every day and PUSH! No one can quit. No one can give up.

My client Robby Robson was a millionaire oilman who is an alcoholic; he gambled his fortune while drunk. He literally lost $500,000 in forty-five minutes while in blackout. Thanks in part to his parents and daughters (Ashley and Amber), he entered a treatment center in South Padre Island, Texas. He showed up at the treatment center thinking he could buy his way out. While there, he learned alcohol was the common nucleus of all his problems.

As part of the 12-step recovery program, he was asked to let God restore him to sanity. Robby told me, "The oilman in me was saying this is a real 'wildcat effort,' and I was full of doubt. I began to lay in bed and force myself to pray, not really believing anyone was hearing me or could care less if they did. I would ask God to take all of my life, the good and the bad, fill me with the Spirit, and make me into the man He wants me to be, and that His will be done and not mine. On the fourth or fifth day after beginning to pray the above prayer, my desire to drink was gone. God got my attention, and changed my life!"

What's your

P
A
S
S
I
O
N
?

EXERCISE

Write one page on what you're passionate about.

FEAR kills

CHAPTER 4

GAF (Guilt, Anger, Fear)

G AF stands for Guilt, Anger, and Fear. A lot of the time when a person is an addict, their heart is filled with guilt, anger, and/or fear. More often than not, they may feel all three emotions, which lead to confusion, regret, and bondage. For any person, they cannot change or heal what they do not acknowledge. This is why it is important to explore the cause of the pain in one's heart.

My friend Brad Reeves suffered not only from guilt, anger, and fear, but also shame. He tells his story of conquering the demons that come with alcoholism. Brad is my neighbor who is an amazing family man who gives back to the community. I never asked his story until recently. It is beautiful how God works as he describes the following "civil war":

It all began in 1984, when as a high school student, I traveled with my church youth group to Leadville, Colorado, to take part in a mission trip. I have always loved the mountains because there I marvel at creation and am reminded how big God is. While on the mission trip, we spent one day hiking to the top of Mt. Elbert. That same day I gave my life to Jesus Christ and asked Him to be my Savior. Later that same week, I began drinking alcohol at a very young age. So goes my "story of Job."

For the next twenty years, I progressed in my faith and in my drinking. I would often pray for God to "finish the good work He started in me," then continue to wander in the wilderness and the world. It's a tough go when you have a heart full of God and a belly full of alcohol. By all accounts, I was a first-class alcoholic for those twenty years. To others, I was the "life of the party." To many, I didn't have a problem. Yet inside, I was riddled with guilt, anger, fear, and shame. The last five years of my drinking, I struggled mightily, and was absolutely conflicted—hating the idea of drinking, but unable to stop.

I tried on several occasions, both independently and with the help of AA programs, but couldn't put together a year of sobriety. When I did, I'd often replace it with some other addiction—even running and exercise.

On February 18, 2004, I had a moment of clarity. I had been sixty days sober when I crashed. I was on a business trip in Florida, had gone to dinner and abstained from drinking, and retired early to bed. Then, in an almost out-of-body experience, I crawled out of bed, got dressed, and went to find a bar. I hit it hard, blacked out, and missed my flight in the morning. A business partner and brother in Christ was on the trip with me. When we returned to Dallas, he took me to a Celebrate Recovery meeting at his church, and for the first time, for me, AA met scripture, hymns, and Jesus. Now, almost ten years later, I am sober and proudly work with others to help them through their struggles. I have the tools to PUSH! myself and others through my spiritual life and the knowledge I gained from my own experience as well as Celebrate Recovery. About a year or two into my sobriety, I was finally able to grasp the concept of grace. God's grace is about taking the absolute worst day of your life and making it the absolute best.

Another example of guilt, anger, and fear leading to addiction involves another client, whom I will call Joe Bob.

He was eaten up with guilt. He was a terrible father and worse husband. My friend Bobby B., who worked at La Hacienda Treatment Center, brought him in. Joe Bob was at the end of the progressive disease of alcoholism. He was drunk on blue Listerine, which tells you how bad of shape he was in. Joe Bob had been to seven treatment centers. He was in and out of AA. He was one guilt-ridden, shame-filled man, and he carried himself that way. The only thing consistent with him was his give-up attitude driven by fear. He was mad at God, and it wasn't working for him.

After I spent five minutes with him, I learned he never dealt with the guilt in his heart at any of the treatment centers in which he participated. He didn't understand that the only way he was going to get sober was to heal his heart, then work on a recovery plan. In addition to inpatient treatment, we placed him in a life skills program to deal with his guilt.

Fortunately, Joe Bob acknowledged his guilt and shame and had the opportunity to deal with it in a mature, safe fashion. All of us in the program witnessed the miracle. Joe Bob got sober and became president and CEO of a large medical software program. Like many alcoholics and drug addicts, all he needed was a safe platform to deal with his heart.

The problem with Joe Bob is similar to that of a majority of the clients that I work with, including the teens and young adults. All of them are dealing with guilt, anger, or fear (GAF). Some are dealing with it at more extremes than others. For example, I deal with so many teens that are deeply angry at their parents for being absent. They feel abandoned as their parents are hard at work trying to make sure their children don't have it as hard growing up as they did. The parents try to smother the teen's anger by throwing money at them. This makes the kids even more mad, as it does not fill the holes in their hearts. Then the addictions set in, and the vicious GAF cycle is at work destroying the family unit.

Fear sets in as well. As the addiction is being fueled by guilt and anger, fear of not healing the addict fills the family unit. It is interesting to me how fear of failure and fear of success play such an important role with the addict. It is common for an addict to get comfortable living a healthy recovery program, and then, all of a sudden, they set themselves up to fail as a result of their fear of success. For some reason, they drink alcohol or use drugs because they are doing so well. It is important for them to pick themselves up immediately and identify the "why" and jump right back into their program. People who experience fear of failure usually lean toward perfection and work extremely hard not to fail.

People who have fear of success usually are the ones who set themselves up to fail.

Living in the penitentiary becomes easy for most inmates. They learn how to do their time. Just like living in addiction, it becomes easy; it's the only way an addict knows how to live—the lazy way. They learn to fear success and many times will commit a crime after their release so they can return to someone telling them how to live.

Everyone in the family is at a loss as to why they cannot fix the addict. It should be simple, right? Just stop drinking and doing drugs and everyone and everything will be all right. Unfortunately, it doesn't work that way; the GAF cycle has to be dealt with by professionals and the family has to get involved as a team in order to successfully break this cycle.

Fear is different. It is an emotion that must be removed so you can make choices from a position of strength instead of from a position of weakness. Fear is an emotion that begins with a lack of faith. The opposite of fear is strength. We get strength from God. He blesses us with the courage and strength to make the right choices. He gives us the power, love, and sound mind to make the right decision every time. He fills the holes in our heart with love, strength, peace, and joy. He wants us to have a different life than that of a victim. He wants us to be winners, not losers; joyful, not depressed; peaceful, not angry; forgiven, not guilty; of sound mind, not confused; and powerful, not weak.

Fear is a driver of a lot of bad decisions. Fear causes people to react; they pull instead of PUSH! What fears do you have to overcome?

It is my job to give clients strength and hope. It is my job to give them the willpower to PUSH! forward. Also, my passion is to draft the perfect treatment team for each client and assign the various duties to each member. This is where I get my heart filled. I feel it is totally the lawyer's job to follow up and monitor the client's treatment via review plans provided by the treatment facility. I have never had a relationship with a treatment provider that didn't want to work with me as a lawyer and a counselor.

GAF – JOURNALING

With this exercise you will learn to track your feelings with action items to help you live a healthy lifestyle. Use this format to create your own daily journal.

Write – "THIS IS THE MOST IMPORTANT TIME OF MY LIFE!"

Write – the date with the day of the week on the top of a blank sheet of paper.

Write 1 through 10 for a task list.
1. Spend time with kids on homework.
2. Be careful with whom I share confidence.
3. Work out on a regular basis.
4.
5.
6.
7.
8.
9.
10.

Write one paragraph – I feel guilty when _____. Be specific with names and dates. For example, I feel guilty when my friend Job breaks confidence with me.

Write one paragraph – I feel fear when _____. Be specific with names and dates.

Write one paragraph – I feel happy when _____. Always end with proud or happy.

CHAPTER 5

Victim

There is a time in some people's lives when they have a defining moment when things change. It happens in an instant ... *bam*! It can be the loss of a loved one, sexual molestation, rape, watching a murder, divorce, abortion, physical abuse by a parent, cancer, loss of a job, loss of a friend, or whatever the defining moment is for you. Immediately, things change and your world as you know it is turned upside down. When you wake up the next day, you feel different, act different, look different, and living life becomes a challenge.

Has it ever happened to you?

There becomes a hole in your heart that has to be filled because you cannot handle the pain. Your choices are changing in order to fill this hole. You turn toward drugs, alcohol, or food. You may become depressed, and you may choose to live alone instead of surrounding yourself with good, God-loving people. Jobs or school are difficult to maintain. You continue to drink more, drug more, or eat more to fill the pain in your heart.

The pain in your heart is guilt, anger, or fear. You can't run from it and the only way to heal it is to acknowledge it. This is a personal choice. Just like picking up a pencil off your desk, it is a choice. Once you choose to look at it and deal with it, you have made a choice to not live like a victim and to become accountable for the way you treat yourself, those around you, and your children. You are choosing the ultimate win/win choice for you, which is freedom in your heart.

After you choose to pick it up and look at it, the next step is forgiveness. This is difficult. The road traveled to peace always goes through forgiveness. You either have to forgive yourself to heal guilt or forgive someone else for the anger that you feel. It is not easy, and there is no magic dust that we can sprinkle over your head to cure it. Sometimes it is easier if you remind yourself that you are not forgiving them for them, but you are forgiving them for *you*. Forgiveness is about you and the way you feel and the way you feel in your heart. It is a choice: do you want to feel anger, or do you want to feel at peace?

If you get stuck in victim mode it is hard to be successful at anything. Why PUSH! when I always FAIL? It is difficult to trust people. It's hard to establish solid friendships. No one wants to hire a victim to lead their organization. Someone might feel sorry for a victim, but they will not have confidence in the victim to be strong, courageous, and capable of leadership.

Over the course of my career, I have experienced and seen almost everything. I have seen families full of hope and resilience, and I've seen the darkest side of human tragedy. I have worked with young people whose lives have been impacted by drugs, addiction, abandonment, and loss, and I have witnessed first-hand the power of words. When I am involved in a trial, fighting for someone's life, the words I say could make the difference between life and death. When debate is your business, you are paid to find the right words. Words matter.

One of the things I do when I represent clients is to help people stop living the life of a victim. Yes, they were victimized. But they do not have to continue being a victim. Sooner or later, one has to become accountable for his or her life. They have to become accountable for their choices, including their emotions and the way they feel.

When I decided to write this book, I knew that I wanted to share my success and mentor others, and also to convey the decades of powerful experiences that I have had. In studying human nature I have discovered that most people who are facing the trauma of a trial are either angry, full of guilt, or full of fear. If they can wipe that slate clean, they are free. If they hang on to the title of victim and define themselves that way, they never get freedom. They are trapped in a victim mentality, and they are not afraid to pull the victim card. I try to get them to let go of that, so they can start over again, build a new life, and rip off the rearview mirror.

My life has not been perfect. In my youth I had seasons of challenge, growth, and freedom. It is the sum of all those experiences—not just my strengths but in the weak seasons, too—that allow me to relate to my clients when they're in the struggle. Because I have been there, I see things from God's point of view. There's more to the person sitting across the conference table in front of me than his struggles with life, addition, or the law.

I wanted to write this book to not only change lives, but also to encourage you to help others move toward their goals and dreams along the way. You might just be that only voice in the wilderness that they hear. You might be the one person who helps this person "out of a ditch."

Life is a challenge in which people have to learn to rise up and continually grow, give, love, and serve. Will you rise to the challenge? The challenge is about making you a stronger person until you have reached the potential or destiny that God has for your life.

But you cannot do that if you are stuck in limiting or destructive beliefs. These limiting beliefs are nothing more than negative tapes. It may be compared to a boom box playing a tape over and over. If you go on feeling like a victim, and believing you are a victim, you ARE a victim. People with limiting beliefs live their life in a box. This box is a comfort zone. It is a cold, dark box full of deep, dark secrets. Successful people live "outside of the box." They live their dreams. They take calculated risks that lead to many remarkable discoveries. These winners do not wake up in the morning hearing a limited belief in their brain that tells them, "I am not good enough" or "Why try, it never works out." They wake up hearing, "I am going to live this day to the best of my ability."

I am going to PUSH! and not be PULLED.

Whom do you need to
FORGIVE?

_____

_____

_____

_____

_____

_____

_____

_____

_____

_____

_____

_____

_____

_____

_____

_____

_____

_____

VICTIM EXERCISE
Parental Relationships

What characteristics do you love about your father or father figure in your life? If you do not have a father figure, use God in that place.

_____

_____

_____

What characteristics do you resent about him?

_____

_____

_____

What did you give your father?

_____

_____

_____

What did he give you?

_____

_____

_____

What behavior do you need to keep with your father as an example foryour kids?

_____

_____

_____

What behavior change do you need to break with your father?

_____

_____

_____

What characteristics do you love about your mother or mother figure in your life?

_____

_____

_____

What characteristics do you resent about her?

_____

_____

_____

What did you give your mother?

_____

_____

_____

What did she give you?

_____

_____

_____

What behavior do you need to keep with your mother as an example for your kids?

_____

_____

_____

What behavior do you need to break with your mother?

_____

_____

_____

CHAPTER 6

Forgiveness

I've seen, many times in my career, how the seed of not being able to forgive destroys lives. Nothing good comes from holding on to bitterness.

Winners practice the power of forgiveness. This is the tough one for me. I have to remember when God washed the feet of all the disciples, he washed *all* their feet. He was not selective. He did not say, "Oh, I will wash your feet because you did this for me," or "I will not wash your feet because you did not do this for me. He washed all their feet and passed the towel to dry them. He even washed Judas's feet ... and Judas was was the ultimate traitor who sold Jesus out for money. Humbly, He kneeled down in a subservient position and washed their feet.

I envision the Lord handing me the towel to wash and then dry the feet of those of those who have violated me in my life. It is a powerful exercise. Anger is the poison that kills you while it is directed at someone else. Forgiveness is not a verbal exercise. It is heartfelt. I tell clients who have suffered major loss that they may want to lay their anger at the feet of Jesus. I do not know what else to say or where else to send you. It is just so heart-wrenching to experience major losses here on earth, yet that is what some people face.

No one is guaranteed seventy or one hundred years on earth. Life is a random series of events, and there are tragedies, obstacles, and challenges along the way. I have faced my own share, including the premature and surprising death of my brother, Charlie.

The best way to get back at someone who violated you as a child or mistreated you in some way is to forgive them. People usually cannot grasp this principle. They respond, "You're telling me that I need to forgive someone who raped me?" I say, "Yes ma'am, but the forgiveness is for you and not for them." As long as you have anger in your heart for them, they are winning, and what they did to you is affecting the way you live your life. Forgiveness is not approval. It is just letting go. It removes the power someone or something has over you because you have let it go, essentially eliminating it from your from your mental and psychological life.

Forgiveness is the pathway to freedom in your heart.

Once you truly forgive someone, you are free to live your life the way God intended you to live. How can you achieve your business goals and dreams and be a good partner in any relationship if you are tethered to bitterness? If there is something in your past that is causing you agony—a relationship that ended badly or a conversation that impacted your soul—be sure to silently, and maybe even in person, offer forgiveness.

Once your heart is free by the act of forgiving, then you are capable of filling the void with powerful characteristics of winners. For instance, winners and champions have bonding power. This is the ability to get people to sign on to your dreams. It compares to passion. My friend and legal mentor, John McShane, always listens to me. He has a way of helping me find peace in every issue that I discuss with him. I know that when I confide in him, he has my best interest in mind every time. John has had a huge impact in the entire Dallas legal community by creating safe environments for lawyers to heal. He is not afraid to intervene with any lawyer fighting alcohol or drug addiction.

Great trial lawyers like John McShane have bonding power. They have the unique ability to get twelve people to buy into their position in five days. They have never met these people before and they know very little about them. Yet they can persuade them to buy into their position in five days. Very few lawyers have this ability.

There are several key traits of winners, and my point in outlining them for you here is to illustrate that there's a distinct difference. And the distinction is as different as a red car or a purple one. You have the ability to choose. It is as different as choosing a home on a beach or a cabin in the mountains. You have the ability to choose. If you want to be a winner, you also have the ability to choose.

You can choose to create a successful life. Just make a decision to walk in the habits and traits of winners. Learn what they learn, and do what they do.

EXERCISE

Whom do you have to forgive?

_____

_____

_____

_____

_____

_____

_____

What do you have to forgive them for?

_____

_____

_____

_____

_____

_____

_____

_____

_____

God doesn't want you to

FEEL the spirit
of fear,

He wants you to

FEEL the power, love,
and sound mind.

PART 1

What specific action do you need to implement to forgive yourself?

_____

_____

_____

Why do you deserve to be forgiven?

_____

_____

_____

What happens to you if you don't forgive yourself?

_____

_____

_____

PART II

Whom do you need to forgive?

_____

_____

_____

What specific action do you need to implement to forgive them?

_____

_____

_____

Why do you need to forgive this person who has violated you?

_____

_____

_____

What happens to you if you don't forgive them?

_____

_____

_____

CHAPTER 7

Stop/Start

You cannot wake up every morning and PUSH! if you are confused and unfocused. You absolutely must remain focused on your goal, your family, your dream, and your success. You have to stop doing things that distract you and start doing things to keep you focused so you can complete the task.

What is it you have to let go of or "Stop?" How do you need to let go of the things that do not serve you? How do you "Start" acting from a positive set of values and beliefs?

Everything starts with our belief systems. If you have limited beliefs, you will live a limited life. If you start believing in yourself, then you will have a fulfilling life. People who do not believe in themselves will struggle until they are either inspired by someone who does or until they change their belief system.

As I have written, winners and champions have definite characteristics that separate them from the rest of the pack. One distinct quality, though, is that they believe. They believe in success. They believe they can achieve. They believe in something bigger than themselves.

It does not just happen that someone is a winner. It is a learned process. You may call it what you want. Growth, recovery, a journey, or discovery, but just know that becoming a winner is truly a process of growth. My wife, Sanka, is a winner. My business partner, Fred Lowder, is a winner. My coach, Tony Jeary, is a winner. My writer, Tammy Kling, is a winner. My friend, Bobby B, is a winner. Winners are givers that are difference makers. They are high-energy achievers who want more in their lives. People want to be around them, which may be good and bad. Sometimes opposites are attracted to winners, so boundaries must be defined. This means keep the good in and the bad out.

Ah, you say, I've never thought of it that way!

That is right. If you want to win, I am coaching you to step up and align yourself with winners. These will be people outside your comfort zone and they will stretch you immensely. But if you are a winner, beware of energy drainers when you are mentoring others. Mentor, but be cautious not to let people suck the life out of you. Winners hang out with winners.

Winners are hard-working people who stay true to the formula. It starts with self-awareness. Winners know the choice of being a winner starts in them.

You have to take care of yourself before you can take of others. It is a basic principle of life and it is the truth. When you board an airplane, the flight attendant begins the survival instruction by telling you to first put the oxygen mask on yourself, then your child second. It sounds selfish at first, but it makes sense. Winners approach life that way. That is, take care of yourself so you can take care of others.

Again, it all goes back to what we talked about in chapter two. Life is about choices.

You can make a choice to be a winner or a choice to be a loser. It is a powerful gift that God has given us and life is a series of daily choices. Each day, make the decision to finish strong. Make healthy choices, and then make a commitment to stay focused on those choices any time you are presented with an alternative. Your life is uniquely yours.

What does success mean to you? I have made a choice not to drink alcohol for the last twenty-one years. Just like I made the choice to pick up a pen and start writing this book. It is a choice. I am proud of my choice. Sometimes, a glass of wine sure sounds good, but I choose not to drink. In my law firm, I witness the destruction people face for choosing to drink too much alcohol or take illegal drugs. Some say that God's gift of freedom of choice results in sin in the world. It is a hard point to argue. For me, life is just easier when I am clear-headed and not under the influence of anything.

Winners are committed to achieving their goals. And because of that, they are aware of the bigger picture. I have noticed that successful people are timely, and they also respect other people's time. They are responsible, but most importantly, they are committed to finishing the task at hand.

Think about the friends you know that are committed to God first, family second, and their job, third. Chances are, you like them, because they are givers, not takers, and they are winners in life, love, and family.

The BE is the last part of "balance, believe, and be" for a reason. It is easy to say, Just be; live your life. That is the reason I like to say PUSH! I would much rather use the strategy of being offensive in life than defensive. PUSH! rather than be PUSHed—and somewhere in between lies a happy medium. Unfortunately, to get to this offensive strategy, you have to have a free heart and heal from any defining moments that have had a negative impact in your life.

Each one of us has defining moments in our lives. What are yours? How are you going to learn to stop self-defeating behavior and learn to BE? Specifically, how can I lay the drama down and really lead a responsible life plan? There are positive defining moments and negative ones. Let me start by saying that when I coach my people, I approach this subject in a pretty interesting way.

I ask them to journal on the specifics of the defining moment. I tell them to write about the incident, including how old they were, where they were, what happened to them, and how it changed their life. I tell them to include their feelings in their journal. At the same time, I tell them to include the action steps they need to take to heal the negative feelings and support the positive feelings.

It is a powerful exercise for the participants.

I have them write how they are going to be accountable to themselves, their families, and their friends. The end result? They were no longer victims. They were champions. I would have them write at the end of each day of journaling how they were proud of themselves for the work they were doing.

We've all heard the war stories of others, recounting life's tragedies in the battlefield. Logically, we know the dark valleys are hard to get out of, but through effort and time, we keep forging ahead. Onward and upward. One day at a time. One step at a time. What appears a simple formula for the bystander can resemble a calculus formula for the overcomer. Journaling is a powerful tool that is simple but liberating, especially when used over a period of time.

When a person sees no end in sight and no options, then logic tells us there has got to be an easier way. Accountability and honesty is a good place to start.

If we use the analogy of a skyscraper, there are really only two very distinct floors that stand out among all those numbered in the elevator.

The Basement and the Penthouse.

If we attach the negative to the Basement and the positive to the Penthouse, you can track which way you are heading and get a sense of how far you will have to travel to get there.

Being honest with yourself requires accepting the vulnerability of human error.

Ask yourself: "Where is this adversity taking me?" and "Am I going up (overcoming) or going down (defeating)?"

Feeling trapped, without an escape in sight, you begin banging on the doors of your life; everyone will be witnessing your panic, they will hear you, but they will be unable to help.

Remain conscious and observe this adversity. Avoid giving in to the temptation to check out, deny, or allow ego to consume you.

By allowing these habits, you get stuck between floors, and the character of regret takes over. Then you are unable to go anywhere with your life.

How about you? Are you going to make the decision to overcome and rise to the challenges and joys of life?

EXERCISE
Start/Stop

What behavior do you need to Stop?

_____

_____

_____

How is this behavior keeping you from success?

_____

_____

_____

What positive action do you need to START?

_____

_____

_____

How will this change in behavior change your life?

_____

_____

_____

CHAPTER 8

Trust

When someone has been the victim of something that had value in their lives, it is not uncommon to develop an inability to trust. If you were betrayed, abused, or deceived, chances are you lost trust in whoever did that to you. Trust is usually the first trait to go once a person is victimized. Victims of a defining moment lose trust—not only in the perpetrator, but in *themselves*. Interesting how that works. That is, a victim will quit trusting themselves as well as others. You may have lost faith in humanity, or you may have lost faith in yourself. A lack of trust can impact relationships and create conflict.

Addressing the root of trust issues is important to recovery in all areas of your life. It is difficult to teach someone to trust again. It takes time as well as an awesome therapist. My therapist, Betty Lindsey, did an amazing job teaching me how to trust—even her. In my initial consultation with her I told her that I needed to go to a listening class; I also believed I had a hearing problem. She chuckled and told me I was in the right place. Seven years later, I learned to trust myself again.

Trust involves a commitment because you must make up your mind that you are willing to connect with others, and to build. If you trust, you are good at building, and not tearing down. Trust is required in commitment.

What is it you are committed to?

If you are committed to winning in all areas of your life, you will. If you are absolutely determined to be a winner in life, love, relationships, finances, and business, how can you lose? You will be dedicated to making the right choices no matter what anyone else around you does.

Spouses that are committed to their marriage do not cheat. They are loyal. They do what is necessary to protect the sanctity of the marriage. They fight for each other. They protect each other. They listen to each other. They are friends. They trust each other. When a spouse cheats, there is usually a line of dead bodies left behind. The kids feel they have been cheated as well, and should be included in the body count.

Trust and commitment go hand in hand.

Workers that are committed to their jobs are loyal. They are creative to make the business better. They are honest with their managers because they care. They do whatever they can, whenever they need to, to make their business successful.

But even the most successful people sometimes have doubt. Maybe you doubt yourself, or you do not trust that you can achieve something. That is when fear starts to creep in, and negative self-talk and doubt fill your head. In that situation, you have got to have a plan. At the end of each chapter, there are exercises to help you reset your mind when doubts creep in, but one method I use is to have a pre-set script that plays in my head. It helps me face frustration, challenge, and obstacles head on. When I am about to go into a challenging trial and I am uncertain how things will go, I remember Psalm 27. It is a perfect reminder to trust.

Even if you have fears, doubts, or mistrust about humanity, you can trust in God. David wrote this in the darkest days of his life when he needed help. He cried out to God. Haven't we all been there?

The LORD is my light and my salvation—whom shall I fear? The LORD is the stronghold of my life—of whom shall I be afraid? When evil men advance against me to devour my flesh, when my enemies and my foes attack me, they will stumble and fall. Though an army besiege me, my heart will not fear; though war break out against me, even then will I be confident. One thing I ask of the LORD, this is what I seek: that I may dwell in the house of the LORD all the days of my life, to gaze upon the beauty of the LORD and to seek him in his temple. For in the day of trouble he will keep me safe in his dwelling; he will hide me in the shelter of his tabernacle and set me high upon a rock. Then my head will be exalted above the enemies who surround me; at his tabernacle will I sacrifice with shouts of joy; I will sing and make music to the LORD. Hear my voice when I call, O LORD; be merciful to me and answer me. My heart says of you, "Seek his face!" Your face, LORD, I will seek.

Do not hide your face from me, do not turn your servant away in anger; you have been my helper. Do not reject me or forsake me, O God my Savior. Though my father and mother forsake me, the LORD will receive me. Teach me your way, O LORD; lead me in a straight path because of my oppressors. Do not turn me over to the desire of my foes, for false witnesses rise up against me, breathing out violence. I am still confident of this: I will see the goodness of the LORD in the land of the living.

Wait for the LORD; be strong and take heart and wait for the LORD.

If you are totally honest with yourself, you trust very few people in your life. I have maybe three people that I really trust. This is my inner sanctum, which I call my first layer of friends. I can tell them anything. I can always depend on them for honest feedback. They are the ones who have my back when I go to battle.

Then I have my second layer of people who I trust, but I do not let them in all the way. It is not that I have a superficial relationship with them; I just do not know whether I can trust them all the way. My gut tells me: "I wouldn't tell them, Brett, because I don't know if you can trust them all the way." This is fine as long as you know the game. Don't you find that your gut, that is, our natural instinct to act or not to act, is right 99 percent of the time? So the bottom line is, don't tell them, tell God.

The third layer of people is people whom I have to be

around even if I don't trust them. The key to this type of involvement requires you to rely on the mature side of your brain. It would be easy for you to smart off or be sarcastic every time that you are around this group of people, but the best tool to employ is *keep your mouth shut*. Stay quiet. Don't fuel the fire and give them any information about your life. Trust me: it is a hard strategy, but you are usually better for it.

EXERCISE

Write about your first layer of people you trust and why.

_____

_____

_____

Write about your second layer of people you trust and why.

_____

_____

_____

Write about your third layer of people you don't trust and why.

_____

_____

_____

CHAPTER 9

Choices

You cannot wake up every morning and PUSH! unless it is your choice.

How will we lead our kids and ourselves? It is an intentional decision, each day. A choice to PUSH!

Champions make good choices. They choose to wake up every morning and PUSH! The choices they make tend to be continually positive and progressive, taking them in forward motion toward their dreams.

Throughout your life you will be given the opportunity to make a lot of choices. Some negative, some positive. Choose carefully. Even the smallest choice can be the thread that unravels your life.

Over and over again I have seen how one bad choice can lead to a lifetime of distress. Sometimes it is just a non-choice that causes problems—for instance, a lack of attention to a problem at home, or a lack of communication with a teen. When work is placed above family time, often it is an unintentional "choice."

In this world, there are so many choices and options that it can be confusing and nearly impossible to make the right one. Now imagine being a teenager with an underdeveloped brain, faced with the same choices.

Can we all agree that there is a major communication breakdown between most parents and the current generation of techie children? How many of you have been driving down the road with the kids in the car, and when you asked them a question, you received no response? For example, you ask, "Hey kids, would you like to get some ice cream?" No response. Then, you, as a curious parent, lovingly ask your kids again whether they would like to get some ice cream. No response. As you feel "less than" and "frustrated" as to the lack of response, you turn your head to discover your kids busily working their phones or iPads. Truth is, they never heard a word. This scenario, my friends, is a global communication breakdown.

We have to fit in with the tools our kids use, and yet we have to manage them well into our lives. It is a choice. It is not about taking stuff away. The kids will only resent that. It is about managing your time together as a family and nurturing relationships.

The age of technology benefits America as it provides a wealth of information and opportunity. The positive is that you want your children to benefit and be able to adequately use computers and PDAs. The negative is that our kids lose communication tools such as speaking, listening, grammar, and diction. They learn to live in their head and not their heart, which creates a barrier between parents and children. They lose their passion and desire to PUSH! by hiding in their world of technology.

Kids would rather look at their PDAs than tell you how their day at school went or how they enjoyed the movie. We all fall into that trap of escapism, though. Not just the kids. Isn't it tempting to look at your cell phone during dinner or a meeting, or to check email one last time? It takes real discipline not to. Recognizing how our small, daily choices (how we communicate with our kids, how we manage our work and home life, etc.) affect our lives can reap the biggest reward. And when we do make bad decisions (large or small), it is time for a course correction.

We all make bad choices. But it is how you recover from them and how you handle the majority of them that matters. The best advice I received from my legal mentor, John McShane, thirty years ago, is that no matter how hard it gets, put your armor on every morning, and go to work. PUSH!

I've seen how one DUI has led to a driver's license suspension, which led to a job loss, which led to fighting about money at home, which led to financial and marital distress, which led to a divorce, a foreclosure, custody battles, addiction, more drinking, and even a downward spiral to homelessness. It all starts somewhere. People who end up facing criminal charges weren't born with them. Remember in Jeremiah 1, when God said, " . . . before you were born, I knew you"? You were born a champion. And, unfortunately or fortunately, God gave us all the free will to make our own decisions. How well have you managed that responsibility?

As a society, we haven't managed it that well. In the United States, approximately one in every thirty-one adults (7.3 million) are behind bars or being monitored on probation or parole. Can you imagine that? Seven million people!

Regardless of the reason, 30 percent of young Americans have arrest records before the age of twenty-three. And I can tell you from experience that how that initial arrest record is handled can dictate the course of a young person's life. Will they be represented and rehabilitated? Will they have a second chance at their dreams? I have seen many young people who have gone on to live fully restored lives—clients who have transformed their lives to raise families, give back to society, and earn strong incomes to support their wives and children.

But the only way that happens is when they decide to make the right choice. A lot of people say that someone has to hit rock bottom before they can get help to start making the right choices. It is hard for me to support that view in this day in time. Why? Today's drugs are more potent and extreme than in other generations. Also, I do not think it is fair to pawn off your problems on someone else. It is not right to send a person making horrible choices back to society when they could kill someone. This means it is not fair to say, "Well, if Joe goes out and kills someone while driving his car, maybe he will finally start making better choices."

My nephew, Chad, killed himself at sixteen. He went into a dark room and put his head on the barrel of a .22 rifle and pulled the trigger. It was one of the darkest days of my life. I miss him. I would have never thought I would have been part of him donating his organs at sixteen. There is a part of me that feels guilty that I did not do enough to help him. I knew he was having mental issues, but I did not do enough to help him. He was making bad choices. Maybe if I would not have quit on him, it could have been different. I have learned from this horrific loss, and I will never turn from someone in need of help again until God tells me it is best for me to walk away.

See, when someone makes the choice to commit suicide, there are other choices that have to be made by the survivors. Survivors have to choose how they are going to live after a suicide. They do not understand or comprehend why you killed yourself. They feel guilty and always wish they would have done more. Also, there are always things left unsaid between the survivor and the deceased. Survivors always look back and wish they had the opportunity to tell the deceased how much they loved them, how they would do anything to help them see the desire to live again, and how they are mad at them for killing themselves. Next, are they going to live as grief-stricken victims, or are they going to live as mature, strong people who have a special place in their heart for you? With my family, my mother never recovered from the loss of her grandson. She was broken, and then when my brother passed with cancer, it was too much for her.

That is OK. But when you have children who depend on you or surviving siblings, you have got to recover for them. I like to say it is time for you to put your "big girl" pants on and move on. It is a choice how YOU live your life. You have to make the responsible choice of waking up every morning, and make a conscious decision to PUSH!

My wife, Sanka, was diagnosed with breast cancer four months after my brother died. She didn't give up. She fought the fight. I never forget when she told me, "Hey! I'm not going anywhere! You're crazy if you think I am going to leave you with my two little girls to raise!" She was there for me and our family when Charlie had died. Her choice was to kick cancer and beat it. She had an unbelievable winning spirit that was intoxicating to everyone around her. There are two parts to fighting cancer: mental and physical. She took care of her part and the doctors took care of theirs. Her winning spirit speaks of her positive choices when looking at a major obstacle thrown her way. She not only made the choice to PUSH!, but also to hit the ball right out of the park.

EXERCISE
Choices

Write about the worst choice you ever made in life and how it changed your life.

_____

_____

_____

Write about the best choice you ever made in life and how it changed your life.

_____

_____

_____

CHAPTER 10

Free Will

You cannot wake up every morning and PUSH! unless you have a positive attitude.

God gave us free will. He gave us a brain. He gave us the ability to make choices and decisions, and it all began with Adam and Eve in the Garden of Eden. There they were, in paradise, and they even messed it up back then. It makes you wonder: is free will a gift or is it a responsibility? I think it is a little of both.

Free will is a gift because God did not have to give it to us. It is a responsibility because it is so powerful that it has to be managed. Seriously, think about it . . . why did 9/11 happen? Because terrorists had the free will to make a plan, learn to fly planes, and crash them into the twin towers, killing thousands of Americans. God gave us all the free will to make our decisions, choices, and career paths in life. Our free will starts every morning when we decide what to wear in the morning. God can help you pick it out, but you make the choice. It is no different than when Eve ate the apple and gave it to Adam and said, "Here: have some of this."

Successful people manage responsibility well. They are difference makers. I see a lot of people make money, but they do not know how to manage it responsibly. More than once, I have witnessed these people commit crimes because they could not manage success.

Our free will and decision-making process can be affected by the way we were raised. Life-defining moments or mental or emotional disease may also affect the way we make choices. There are a lot of psychobabble interpretations of scientists who write that free will is based on neural differences. I disagree. I believe that everyone has tapes that may affect the way we make decisions, but these negative tapes may be broken by personal choice and replaced with positive tapes that lead to better choices.

Free will will be treated more responsibly when you act on positive tapes rather than personal tapes. For example, a 25-year-old man may rape a person and use the excuse that he raped because he was raped when he was younger. He may argue that his free will was impacted by this traumatic event and that is all he knows—i.e., rape. Actually, this is a negative tape in his head that was not God-sent. But it's one that he listens to every morning when he wakes up and drags around with him all day. It is like a broken record.

Once people identify the negative audio they are playing over and over again, they are able to achieve a real break-through.

In the example above, it is his choice to replace this negative tape with a positive tape such as "God loves me, and I love everyone around me." And although it might not be that easy, he can learn to manage his free will with responsibility and new positive energy. He can start with baby steps, with small acts of kindness that will develop into easier, smart, every day free-will decisions. Smart, loving counselors, coaches, and psychologists can teach new tapes and assist in replacing old negative tapes by providing new tools.

My coach, Tony Jeary, preaches clarity, focus, and execution. This is the best strategy for countering confusion, fear, and frustration—all of which impact your free will. It is important to begin each day with a plan. This helps manage your free will and decision-making process. If you have a plan, it is easier to stay focused and not get sidetracked. My wife, Sanka, loves to use this tool on weekends. She will sit with me and the girls as a family and ask, "What are we going to do today?" It doesn't have to be a line-by-line approach, but a basic approach to take full benefit of the day and enjoy it. Everyone is on the same page and we all respect each other's time and schedule. Also, everyone is included in the plan, and no one is left out.

I sincerely believe that God wants us to live a life of recovery and not a victim-driven life that will affect our free will.

Emotional and psychological damage may affect one's ability to be responsible with their free will. Depression may affect one's free will. If you do not get anxiety and depression under control, it will take you down. It is difficult to make healthy decisions when you are depressed. Medication and proper psychological assistance are necessary to treat depression and other psychological disorders—all of which can help someone live with healthy, God-centered free will.

Drug abuse and alcoholism have a negative effect on one's free will. Both drugs and alcohol damage the chemical balance in the brain, which not only leads to poor decision-making but also cravings. The progressive aspect of the disease only makes it worse as time goes by.

Fear affects free will. Fear stifles any free will decision-making. You are working "in the box" instead of "outside the box." Fear leads you to feel trapped and affects your free will by creating negative energy. Instead of dreaming, you are dreading. Instead of living by free will, with strength, you are weak and scared. David, the king from biblical times, lived a life of faith, strength, and leadership. He did not worry.

What are the audio tapes going around in your head? Are they negative or are they positive? If they are negative, what do you need to do to transform them to positive tapes? For instance, if you are hearing the negative tape "Why should I try when it never works out," or, "I can't because I am not good enough," then what do YOU need to do as an individual to change the tapes and make them positive? The beautiful gift is that we all have the answers inside of us and the God-given ability to change the tape. It might take adding all new tools in your toolbox, such as strength, forgiveness, self-worth, and faith—or whatever tool you need to conquer the negative tapes. But the beauty will be the miracle you become when you uncover the new you.

EXERCISE
Self-Talk

What negative talk do you wake up with every morning?

_____

_____

_____

How does this negative talk affect the way you live your life?

_____

_____

_____

What positive talk does God want you to hear every morning?

_____

_____

_____

What changes do you need to implement to hear God's voice every morning?

_____

_____

_____

What am I grateful for today?

CHAPTER 11

Dream

You cannot wake up and PUSH! every morning unless you intend to live your dreams.

After you have freed your heart from the past, it is possible for you to enter the dreaming and vision phase of your life plan. Winners and champions are dreamers. How many people in today's society have lost their dreams? Answer: a bunch. I see them on a weekly basis and try to inspire hope and set them back on the right track toward creating a realistic dream toward the future. Dreaming can be a heart-felt moment where you capture the future and answered prayers. Dreaming does not necessarily have to be about having things (biggest house, best car, best job, etc.). It can be about dreaming about your children's wedding or a vacation.

Thomas Edison was a dreamer, and he had a vision. Benjamin Franklin was a dreamer who had a vision. What was going on in his mind when he was flying that silly kite? My friends who are visionaries excite me. They are the ones I go to for feedback. They are the ones who do not think you are crazy when you go to them with an idea.

Winners and champions have VISION. They have the ability to stop and envision the future. What will this look like? What will happen if we do this? What if we do this; what will happen? When we are working a case and we focus on recovery, it is important to help the client create a vision of the future.

It is exciting to be around entrepreneurs who have the ability to envision. It is no surprise that our world relies on entrepreneurs to create jobs when the government cannot. This group of people is fearless. They take risks. They are visionaries. They have to surround themselves with detailed people, as most visionaries could care less how to dot the i's and cross the t's.

What is your vision? What are your dreams?

Let me use an example of my vision and how it affected my life.

After a bit of soul searching and really thinking about what I was passionate about, I discovered what I call "searching for the miracle" in every case that came in my office. I wanted to be part of my clients' journey to freedom rather than just helping them to escape criminal charges.

Searching for a miracle was especially helpful if my clients were suffering from alcohol, drug, or sex addiction. I wanted to help them get free while I was working on their case. This is the recovery defense, and it is a dual-path approach of practicing law. First, the lawyer works on one's case while simultaneously working on their addiction. I guess you could call this therapeutic law, but I like to stick with calling it the recovery defense. It works in both the criminal and civil areas of law.

Once you have witnessed the victory via the recovery defense, it is one of the most rewarding feelings you will ever have. The client is free and healthy and reaps the benefit of his hard work by winning. You are sending a person back into the world with a set of skills and tools instead of sending someone who "beat the system." And winners don't beat the system. Winners become leaders who give back and make the system better.

In the modern day of practicing law, beating the system does not happen very often. Actually, if a lawyer is trying to sell a person on how often he beats the system, the potential client should stand up and leave. He is getting himself into a lose/lose situation. The recovery defense is an out-of-the-box art form that presents various options to the client, judge, juries, and court system. The key to winning is that you have to first paint the vision of the future success, then you have to get everyone to buy into that success by helping your client. Everyone wants to be part of a miracle. How can I help?

Restoration

Most of the time when a client contacts you concerning a criminal case, he is in jail and calling to get released. This is the beautiful part about recovery, because the family members are usually at a point where they are sick and tired of dealing with the client's addiction. They are frustrated, angry, and scared (all at the same time). The lawyer has to be the calm in the eye of the storm.

The best thing to do is to slow things down and get the family in the office. I like to really take my time and learn about the client and the family history. I pray before every meeting and ask the Lord to guide me. He will drop the answers and plan right into your lap. The key is to get everyone on the same plan before I visit with the client in jail. Jail intervention is a much simpler way to get an addict committed to recovery than to get them released first. I start by telling them to be mad at me and not their family, as they are safer right where they are than if on the street doing drugs. I ask them if they want to live or die. I explain how progressive the disease of addiction is and that it will kill them.

Once we come to an agreement as to the recovery plan, I will make a judgment call as to making it stick. If I don't believe the client is committed to recovery, then I will ask the judge to make it a condition of the bond that the client not only attend but complete the inpatient treatment program. If the client leaves the treatment facility AMA (against medical advice), then I will ask the judge to revoke the bond and put the client in jail for treatment. Some would argue this is a conflict of interest, but I handle it in the employment contract and have the client not only waive the conflict but agree with it. I have them sign and initial it. Honestly, I have never had a problem with this strategy in my practice as the client will practice recovery a majority of the time.

Intervention

There are professional interventionists whom you can hire to intervene if a client is not in jail. You should be very selective and careful in selecting an interventionist. I have found myself in dangerous situations by depending on an interventionist who I felt was out of line. This placed all the participants in a dangerous situation. I teach that it is best to interview at least three interventionists before selecting one. You should ask them about their technique, method of intervention, success rate, exit strategy, and professional qualifications to be leading an intervention.

My personal opinion is that a qualified recovery lawyer can handle most interventions at their office. I have handled numerous interventions with addicts in my office over the years. Lawyers usually have the leverage necessary to intervene with an addict and assist in developing an efficient treatment plan. I use Elizabeth Robertson with La Hacienda Treatment Center to assist in facilitating a plan. Lawyers are not psychologists or treatment specialists. They are lawyers. They must decide whether they are going to represent the client and let the professionals do their jobs. I have never seen a lawyer successfully treat an addict for their addiction. It is fine to care about the client and visit them in treatment, but they need to let the pros do their jobs.

EXERCISE

Dreams

Write a paragraph for each of the below:

1. What are your dreams?

_____

_____

_____

2. Have you lost your dreams along the way? If so, why?

_____

_____

_____

3. List the things you would like to do.

_____

_____

_____

4. List the places you would like to see.

_____

_____

_____

5. What would you like to look like?

_____

_____

_____

6. What are your emotional dreams?

_____

_____

_____

7. What are your spiritual dreams?

_____

_____

_____

8. What are you material dreams?

_____

_____

_____

9. What other dreams do you have?

_____

_____

_____

10. What is the legacy you would like to create?

_____

_____

_____

*As you're creating your life plan for yourself and your
family, don't forget to begin with the end in mind.*

VISION.

CHAPTER 12

Peer Pressure

The amazing blessing I receive from my law practice is the opportunity to work with all variations of kids. The one common theme I've experienced is that there are no guarantees to any family that your kids won't get in any trouble or won't get involved with drugs.

NONE.

All you can do is pray, be vigilant about establishing a foundation so that they know how to make the right choices, and know what they're doing and who they are with. And then communicate, communicate, communicate.

Some of the richest kids I have represented have the hardest time getting off drugs because they have not had inner family issues where other family members have experienced drug addiction and the victory of kicking the habit. Also, rich kids have the money to maintain their drug habit, and their parents think their money will simply buy their kids' sobriety. Four treatment centers and numerous attempts at sobriety later, the parents are usually frustrated and angry that their kids are unable to beat the addiction. The sobriety must be a change in heart, which a lot of rich kids do not understand. Rich or poor, it is a human change at the core.

Inner-city kids have witnessed so many generations of their family members dealing with drugs that they do not want to experience the same agony and jail time that Uncle Joe did. That is not always the case, of course, because sometimes the generational habits or curses are passed down, and it becomes a lifestyle issue that is handed down to the kids. They duplicate the behavior. But in a lot of cases I have seen, less wealthy kids would rather take their money to go and buy a pair of tennis shoes rather than drugs. Honestly, inner-city kids get more involved with selling drugs than using drugs. It is their key out of the inner city.

Recently, I had a client, "Joe Bob," who grew up on the rough side of town. He had five arrests for driving while intoxicated over the last ten years. He came to my office with a new DWI, and I noticed that he suffered from hand trembles. He had no self-worth and couldn't look me in the eye. He was filled with guilt and shame from his criminal history. It was obvious that confinement in jail and prison was not the solution. I simply asked him if he had ever admitted to being an alcoholic. He answered, "No." I then asked him whether he was sick and tired of being sick and tired. He said, "Yes."

I then enrolled him into an affordable treatment center, for which his insurance helped pay. He is sober. He has just been honored at his job for achieving major success. All he needed was direction and a little hand-holding. The opportunity for treatment was never presented to him because he was from the inner city, and no one cared. Sometimes all it takes is a caring heart.

Peer pressure is usually the introduction to the drug world. Some kid who your kids are hanging with will smoke a joint and hand it to your kid and say, "Here, try it." The journey begins. Peer pressure is why drug counselors and Alcoholics Anonymous teach that if you want to get sober, you have to change the people you hang with, the places you go, and the things you do. It is a difficult choice the recovering addict must make, but once made, there is light at the end of the recovery tunnel.

Parents have to be one step ahead of the game in order to interrupt the plans of the enemy of your child's heart. Guarding your own heart is not easy, and guarding your child's heart is even harder. You must have a plan. How will you help equip them to fight temptation or peer pressure? Role plays are a great way. Do role plays at home, and present various scenarios. Act like a friend who offers them drugs, and then have your child practice saying, "No thanks, I'm good, dude." Or some other phrase that's an easy, simple way to say no. Rehearse it in advance. Drug awareness program seminars at high schools teach parents to drug test as a way of giving the child an out. Keep the drug test on the counter in the house. The high school student, when asked to participate in drugs, can always say, "My parents drug test, so I can't." Make the "no" easy for your child. We cannot condemn our kids for making bad choices if we haven't prepared them to make good ones.

With my own experience in alcohol recovery, I had to move out of the town in which I grew up, Irving, Texas, and move to Dallas if I really wanted to give myself a shot at not drinking alcohol. I found all my buddies were always trying to put a beer in my hand when I told them I quit drinking. This was twenty-four years ago. When I see them today, they still try to put a beer in my hand. Fortunately, I have the recovery base and tools to choose from when this happens. Teach your kids how to separate from those who continually disrespect their wishes and to separate from those friends who continually make bad choices. Teach your kids that the enemy is not just someone who looks bad. The enemy can be a friend, and it can be yourself. Our own free will can get us into trouble. That is why it's important to PUSH! Praying simply means talking to God when the decisions seem difficult.

In today's world, it is more important than ever to track who your kids are hanging around with. Kids complain that parents are too controlling or that their parents are micromanaging when inquiring about their friends. I respond "great," because I have lost young clients to death because of drugs and peer pressure. It is VITAL to guard your kids and monitor whom they are around. I choose managing who my kids' friends are around over a controlling argument any day of the week. The drugs in today's world are too potent and deadly to not give them the attention needed.

The widespread use of prescription drugs by kids makes

it more imperative that you keep an eye on your kids and friends. Why? It is a more secretive and hidden addiction that can sneak up on your family before you know it. Pill users are cave-dwellers. They go into their little world, take pills, then come back out. It is hard to detect when an adult or child is taking prescription medicines. Sometimes there are no signs.

Parents would be surprised by the parties thrown by teens and the bowl of pills that are placed at the center of the table for anyone to choose from. It happens all the time.

Parents ask me: "What's the key to success in order to keep my kids out of the drug world?" First, I say there are no guarantees. But a good foundation of God and a steady trust and flow of conversation is important. Are you spending time with your kids?

Second, I explain that communication is the key. Kids live in the world of technology. Their communication skills are zero. They live in their head and express themselves via texts, email, and Facebook. They can organize a party of 150 from five different schools in thirty minutes. We have to teach them to talk to us.

This can be done by returning to the major, successful historical tool known as the family dinner. Simply start with a Sunday dinner, but add the rule of no screens. It will be difficult at first, but they will adjust. Trust me, before long, the kids will be asking for a family dinner. Even though they may say they don't want to spend time with the family at dinner, they really do. They crave attention, but they just don't know how to ask for it. Some families have an awesome habit of putting all their phones in the center of the table upside down, making a game to see who can go the entire dinner without touching technology. This works great in a restaurant where everyone, naturally, has brought their cell phones. It can work at home too.

Third, I love to hear when families invoke the team approach. This means we are a team. Look to your left and look to your right. These are the people who care about you. These are the people who will fight for you. These are the people who will take care of you when you are sick. This is your team: each person, each role, each position . . . this is your FAMILY!

Many families practicing the team approach take action steps to build commitment. They take vacations together to spend time learning what is happening in each other's lives. They build vision boards to create dreams for the future. Also, they go to church together, praying with and for each other.

Finally, please remember the phrase: "You're the parent and not the buddy." You can't cultivate love and respect if you're drinking with your kids. Be the authority figure. God set you apart to lead this family, so do it.

You are the boss and not the buddy. I see so many families get in trouble when they take their kids out drinking with them or let them drink alcohol at the home. They respond by telling me they would rather have them drink at home than out in the street. It is illegal to let minor children drink alcohol at home, and you open yourself up to major liability when you serve their friends alcohol as well.

Finally, the families I witness succeed the most are the ones who instill Christian principles and faith into their kids. It is that moment when that little jerk hands your kid a joint when the little voice of protection from God taps your kid on the shoulder and says, "Don't do it." Teach them to talk to God. It's simple. All it means is that they can trust a voice outside of their own. We all need that, because it is impossible to have all of the answers all of the time.

EXERCISE
Goal Setting / Vision Boards

Goal setting should be kept simple. First, pick the areas you wish to grow in. For example, personal goals, financial goals, school goals, spiritual goals, things goals, family goals. Second, decide what you want the goal in that area to be. Third, write three action steps with a time frame of daily, weekly, monthly, or whatever you can achieve.

Personal goal—keep my eye on 195
1. drink tons of water-daily
2. run three miles- three times a week
3. no sugar-daily

Financial goal—to rely on myself for retirement
1. hire financial planner-by end of month
2. contribute to savings-monthly
3. pay income taxes-quarterly

School goal—to obtain a scholarship
1. perform community service-monthly
2. study hard-daily
3. get a job-summers

Family goal—to keep my family healthy and safe
1. plan vacation-two times per year
2. go to lakehouse-two times per month
3. help with kids homework-daily

Vision Boards for the Family

Sit with our family at the dinner table. Each family member takes five minutes to discuss three questions . . .

1. What kind of family do you want to be? Each member discusses this fully before going to question 2.
2. What are the barriers that will keep you from being this type of family? Each member discusses this before moving to question 3.
3. What do you want your family covenant to be? Everyone agrees on family covenant . . . for example: we are a godly, strong, loving family . . . we are a passionate, drug-free family . . . we are a focused, successful, loving family.

You should write the covenant on a tablet and have fun with it. That is, draw on it, paint on it, etc., then hang it for all to see.

CHAPTER 13

Relationships

You cannot wake up every morning and PUSH! unless you are building healthy relationships.

Relationships make the world go round. Sounds corny, but it is true. In my business, relationships are everything. I have to be able to communicate with judges, clients, young people, old people, and other attorneys. If I make someone mad along the way or don't have strong communication skills, it could have a bad outcome. Want to expand on this more?

If you are in business, you need to be good at relationships to be a champion. If you are in a family, you must be good at communicating to be successful in those relationships. And if you are married or want to be, you have got to be skilled in building a relationship. A relationship is simply a one-on-one human connection. At its very core it involves sharing of hearts and minds. A good one can transform your life, but a bad one can destroy it—if you allow it to.

God blessed me big-time with a wife who truly loves and supports me.

My wife, Sanka, is a champion. I prayed for her, and God answered my prayers!

I wrote down all the things I wanted in a relationship on a piece of paper and hid it in my drawer. I wrote the following:

1. I want a giver . . . not a taker in the relationship.
2. I want to be with a woman from a different culture (Sanka is Greek)
3. I want someone who is educated (she received a degree from the University of Virginia, and she is a professional).
4. I want someone who is a professional (she is a national marketing rep for Coca-Cola).
5. I want a friend first.
6. I want someone who puts God first because then I know I will be treated right.

Needless to say, God delivered. Big time.

I coach people that a relationship is directly proportional to the amount of energy each person exerts, and it must be 50/50 to be a healthy relationship. It cannot be 49/51—or there will be problems.

It is possible to maintain a healthy relationship without yelling at one another. Neither Sanka nor I can stand someone yelling at us. In our fifteen years of marriage, neither of us has raised our voices. We might give the "look," but we have never yelled. We disagree on calm, common ground, and I am thankful for that. I am a practicing second-degree black belt in aikido, and if someone starts yelling at me, it won't last long. I can't stand it.

Sanka is a caretaker. I often kid with her that if something happens to me, there will be a line out our front door of MY friends who will attempt to take my place. All my friends love her. She has a huge heart.

She has been there for me for the loss of my nephew, my brother, and my mother. She is a huge supporter. She quietly holds an army up. She has that capability. That is one of the reasons that people love her.

Spouses stick together and support each other.

Sanka was pregnant with Dylan (our youngest) when my brother died in July 2005. She gave birth two weeks after. My daughter's name is Anastasia, (the Greek word for *resurrection*) and she was named after her aunt (Sanka's sister). It was later, when Father Anthony called to check on my emotional state, that I learned the Greek meaning of Anastasia. I wept on the telephone with the priest, the meaning was so fresh and real for me.

Two years later we were having a birthday party at our ranch for my college roommate, John Whitley. It was his 50th. Sanka pulled me in the bedroom as she noticed a large bump on her breast. I assured her it was nothing, but that she should have Dr. Mark Godat check it out.

She went to the doctor, and Dr. Godat thought it might be a cyst, so he tested it with a needle. He directed Sanka to the radiologist to X-ray her breasts. He called us on a Sunday night and told us that Sanka was diagnosed with breast cancer. My heart stopped. All I could think of was my brother and the pain of enduring the loss of him.

We were scared to death as we had already been in one battle with cancer.

Sanka had the winning attitude from the beginning. She was determined to beat cancer as we had two little ones, and they needed their mother. We both put our "big girl" pants on and hit the cancer battle head-on. We had learned from my brother's fight that sitting back and being defensive was not the route we would take. Our strategy was to obtain the best medical care immediately and get the cancer out of her body. We had a team and strategy in place within three days.

Sanka never looked back. She had a positive attitude and went through the numerous surgeries and chemotherapy with amazing stamina. She was not going to lose her battle with cancer. Cancer is a mind game, and she knew she could win with her faith and positive attitude. The *Dallas Morning News* did an article on her about her fight, and her surgeon, Dr. Laidley, often asks Sanka to speak with other patients to coach and counsel them. The moral of the story? Don't give up. Never, ever give up.

I am so proud of her victory. Cancer is behind us, and we claim God's victory. When you face adversity with someone you love, it makes your relationship stronger.

Another important relationship in my life was my friend, Bobby B. He was a top spokesman for AA. I worked with him for twenty years. He worked for La Hacienda Treatment Center. He was the Dallas-area alumni representative and

I handed all my drug and alcohol clients to him to oversee their recovery.

There was nothing that an addict could say to Bobby B. that he hadn't seen or heard. I loved him. He had one leg. He lost the other in prison as he was stabbed multiple times by a gang member. Bobby B. was pronounced dead twice in the Care Flight ride to the hospital. Bobby used to boast that the warden told him he had to pardon him early because it would cost too much to put him back together.

Friends of Bobby B. wheeled him into an AA meeting and the rest was history. He was the number one drug/alcohol counselor in Dallas. He would tell kids who weren't working the deal hard enough to go ahead and quit and go do their time in prison. They would look at him like he was crazy. He had numerous ways of getting their attention. He was a large piece of the miracle puzzle for many recovering alcoholics and drug addicts. I miss him. He would always come to my office, unannounced, at the exact time I would need a shoulder to cry on or an ear to hear. He was God-sent.

I remember one time he came to my office after a young girl we both knew died unexpectedly. She was the lead singer for a choir. Bobby played a role in her recovery. He was so upset. He sat in my office, mad at God, and telling Him to take him and not her. He was crying, yelling, and growling all at once. I admired his honesty. He didn't care about money. He cared about people. He was the Good Samaritan. At his funeral, when I spoke of him as the Good Samaritan, the crowd became vocal, and they all started shouting "He sure was," "Go, Bobby," and "Bobby, we love you!" The preacher who was assigned to the funeral asked me about him, and I told him to sit and listen as I would speak for Bobby. I was proud to stand for him. He is an angel of mine, and I call on him often.

Win/Win Versus Win/Lose Relationships

Who you choose to spend time with will determine how successful you can be. Who are your kids spending time with? Train your children in the way they should go. Ignore the false advice the world gives you about not managing them. They are your kids. They are more important than your money, your investments, or your job.

We make choices about every part of our lives every single day. Choices are made in personal, family, business, and relationship aspects of our lives every minute of the day, and many are life-defining moments. Some are much simpler.

The Webster's definition of choice is "an act of selecting or making a decision when faced with two or more possibilities." So how do we make the right one? Let me start by stating how **not** to make a choice. Choices should not be made based on guilt, anger, or fear. It is always best to invoke the 24-hour rule, which is no action for 24 hours if you need to make a choice and you are angry or scared. You cannot make a win/win decision if you are any of the three.

My favorite Bible verse is in Timothy 1: "God doesn't want us to feel the spirit of fear, but he wants us to feel power, love, and sound mind."

This is important, as God doesn't want us to feel scared, guilty, or angry. These are emotions which need to be managed and balanced when making a choice. I have to remind myself daily that I am not scared and that I need to go to work and make mature decisions on a daily basis whether I want to or not. If I trust God and lean on him and pray for a win/win solution, it will come. I might have to be patient, but it will come, and the right thing will fall out.

Now that we know we need to make choices that are based on power, love, and sound mind, let's go to the next level where we break our choices down to the three categories. Every choice is going to be either win/win, win/lose, or lose/lose. A win/win choice is one where both parties benefit equally. A win/lose choice is one in which one party benefits more than the other, and the choice is made with that in mind. A lose/lose choice is one in which both parties lose by the choice. Honestly, a win/lose choice will lead to a lose/lose result over a matter of time.

Let us implement our new choice-making process in the various aspects of our lives. Personal win/win choices can be life-defining if you learn to implement the process every day. For example, let's say you want to lose weight. If you buy a gallon of ice cream while grocery shopping, you do not make a win/win choice.

If you are stressed about money, a win/win choice could be that you enter "lockdown mode," and keep expenditures to a minimum until you get hold of your budget. Sometimes, it is best to wait for that new suit or new car until you have the money instead of stretching and adding unneeded pressure to yourself. You have got to take care of yourself so you can take care of others. Win/win decisions are ways that you can protect yourself and keep a healthy boundary around you.

Healthy relationships are born from win/win choices. You surround yourself with either givers or takers. Givers want to help you by creating win/win scenarios. Takers only want win/lose from you. They are known for "sucking the life out of you." Do you want to go out with someone who wants you to spend a bunch of money on them, or do you want to go out with someone who wants to learn about you and be your friend?

Win/win decisions in relationships can be difficult because they require you to remove yourself and really think about how to make a win/win choice for another person. This basis is why Dale Carnegie's book *How to Win Friends and Influence People*, published in 1937, has sold fifteen million copies. Carnegie preached if you want to get somewhere in life, you'd better start by learning about other people and their wants. He used the study of the most frequent word in telephone conversations and found, by far, it was the word "I."

My buddy, Mike Studer, is best at this win/win technique in relationships. I listen to him in conversations, and he really spends time to learn about the other person. I tell him he sounds like a lawyer with a witness in cross-examination when he really digs and interrogates to learn about people he just met.

A win/win decision with your spouse and family might concern a vacation. When you feel tired and worn out, a family vacation to a place of their choosing would benefit everyone. Guess what? They are probably tired and worn out too.

My business mentor, Ron Lusk, is the best at creating win/win decisions in business. He calls it having fun. I call it generosity. Before you know it, he has everyone networking for him while letting them benefit as well. It is his way of surrounding himself with healthy people who want to grow.

When you're making any kind of decision in your life, don't forget that it's important to build relationships with people who will help you win.

live one day at a time

EXERCISE

Write one hundred blessings—things you are grateful for. People, places, events, art, beauty, etc.

_____	_____
_____	_____
_____	_____
_____	_____
_____	_____
_____	_____
_____	_____
_____	_____
_____	_____
_____	_____
_____	_____
_____	_____
_____	_____
_____	_____
_____	_____
_____	_____
_____	_____
_____	_____
_____	_____
_____	_____
_____	_____
_____	_____
_____	_____
_____	_____

CHAPTER 14

Boundaries

You cannot wake up and PUSH! every morning if you don't maintain good boundaries.

The most important ingredient for a healthy life plan centers on the concept of boundaries. Boundaries are important for our person as well as our family.

You always hear people say, "It is important to keep healthy boundaries." What does that mean?

The Stalcup Street Smart definition of a boundary means to draw a circle around your body, and always remember to keep the "good in" and the "bad out." It is a simple test that I use daily. Does this person, place, or thing make me better or worse? Does this conversation make me better or worse?

Does this action make me better or worse?

God commands us to guard our hearts in Proverbs 4:23. He tells us, "Above all else, guard your heart, for it is the wellspring of life." He is telling us it is one of the most important things you, as a Christian, can do. That is, GUARD YOUR HEART!

In this era of technology, it is imperative that we take precautions before sharing our hearts as mentors or as friends. Also, it is important that we not only guard our hearts but also our families'.

Sanka and I feel it is important to share our compassion and open our home for people to share our love for mankind. We used to share our gate code, passwords, and various access to our lives with our friends to get into our home. Unfortunately, we had to change our philosophy and rules to draw a boundary around our family . . . to keep the "good in" and the "bad out."

When you let too many people in your world without setting boundaries, bad things happen. Just last week while on summer vacation, we hired a friend to dog sit. It was a win/win situation. We needed the dogs watched, and our friend needed the income.

She was excited to share our home with a friend on a Saturday evening, not realizing boundaries were being broken. We received a desperate and tear-filled phone call about how her friend stole most all of Sanka's jewelry. Fortunately, we were able to recover the property. The moral of the story is: "Guard your heart and the hearts of your family."

Yes, we want to mentor others, but we forget those people we mentor live in a different world. Sometimes, they cannot be brought into our home when our number one mission in life is to keep our family safe. We can share our compassion by maintaining healthy boundaries. We just have to remember to take extra precautions to keep the "good in" and the "bad out."

Keep the "good in" and the "bad out."

EXERCISE
Boundaries

Who brings "bad" into your life? How?

_____

_____

_____

Who brings "good" into your life? How?

_____

_____

_____

How do you need to keep the "good in" and the "bad out"

_____

_____

_____

CHAPTER 15

Conflict

You cannot wake up and PUSH! every morning if you don't have the tools to face conflict.

Families are referred to me because they are in pain. No one brings their kid to a criminal defense lawyer without a history. By the time they walk through my door, there's been a lot of strife and uncertainty that's led them there.

One morning I received a phone call from a parent. He was scared, confused, and at the same time, embarrassed about the predicament that his son's addiction had put his family in. He explained that his teenage son had just been arrested for five aggravated robberies when he committed a home invasion at gunpoint while on a Xanax/alcohol run (a run is drug/alcohol-induced behavior without sleep).

Joe Bob robbed numerous victims at gunpoint expecting drugs to be at an apartment. Not only was he wearing a mask, but he zip-tied the victims' hands at the apartment so they couldn't move. He was arrested driving down the highway an hour later with all the evidence in the car. Joe Bob was either a terrible robber or a drug addict, one or the other.

His father met me at my law office, and he was extremely shaken. He told me how good a boy his son was. Drugs had captured his boy, and he was lost as to what he needed to do. He assured me that he, the parent, was a good person. We prayed together, cried together, and I assured him that we were going to take the worst thing that had happened to his boy and turn it into the best thing. He listened—but didn't believe me at the time.

I immediately visited his son and performed a jailhouse intervention. I asked him if he was sick of jail and wanted to commit to a recovery program. He did. I told him that if he quit recovery or left treatment against medical advice that I would have the bondsmen go off his bond, and he'd be right back where he started. He agreed, and that was the day Joe Bob began a long, hard road to recovery.

He attended La Hacienda Treatment Center, in Texas, for inpatient treatment. Afterward, he attended Mark Houston's outpatient recovery for men, a long-term treatment facility. His parents steadfastly support him; however, recovery is a struggle. He has a hard time grasping recovery for various reasons, but a major one is that his parents have always given him whatever he wanted, and he is having a hard time standing on his own two feet.

He has a willing spirit and a desire to work the program, and when he does, it is like night and day. He goes from a toilet-mouthed punk to a kind, respectful young man. This is what happens when young addicts grasp recovery. You hear the terrible stories of crimes that young addicts commit, but once they grasp sobriety, they are amazing kids.

Chris Raymer, a respected drug/alcohol counselor, says that kids on drugs commit terrible acts, but once they grasp recovery, they can become miracles without an inch of violence in them. He has the scientific data to support this opinion as well as good old street sense from being where the rubber meets the road in recovery. If you've ever been where the rubber meets the road, you understand that it's a place only you can go, and a place only you can get out of. You've got to PUSH! right through and keep on rollin'.

Helping young adults find sobriety is what makes me know I'm in my lane. I enjoy witnessing the freedom won by young adults who defeat addiction. Don't be afraid of the struggle. Don't wilt like a flower. Be a fighter.

The thing you've got to be aware of is that the struggle never comes without a fight. So put on your boxing gloves, and think smart.

Struggles don't need to be considered as barriers as much as they can be viewed as a tool to bring you closer to God. God wants us to lean on Him, and for this to happen, He must many times place struggles in our lives to discipline us. The beautiful fact about this phenomenon is that we will win and overcome struggles if we fight for it, pray, and develop an intimate relationship with God.

Conflict come in three phases. Phase one is conflict that

come at us daily. It might be as small as what to wear to an important meeting because you spilled coffee on yourself, or that the car won't start, and then you're late. This first layer of conflict can be dealt with by daily planning and deliberate action to prevent the small, nagging struggles. Giving yourself more margin time, for instance, is a great and practical way to be prepared for those minor, daily struggles that can impact your mood, and then, an entire day.

Phase two struggles involve FEAR. Many of us struggle with various fears, such as fear of success, fear of failure, fear of intimacy, or fear of trusting people. But fear is a figment of our imagination because it is about the future. God does not want you to feel fear. He wants you to feel power, love, and sound mind. The devil sneaks in and plays games by way of fear. A little voice can be heard in our minds that tells us that we are not good enough, or "Why try for I always fail," or "If I let this person in my heart then they will hurt me." These negative voices that play in our minds are lies that keep us from being free. How do you keep fear out? The way to prepare for this second layer of conflict is to stop fear at the door and start each day with strong, powerful affirmations that give you a mind-set to attack the day.

Phases three struggles is deeper in our hearts and grow into traps. Examples of these traps are alcoholism, drug addiction, eating disorders, depression, or familial issues such as prior abuse or present conflict or misunderstandings. It takes hard work to conquer these traps and negate the negative influence they have on our lives. Tools such as counseling, treatment, journaling, exercise, or goal-setting can lead to freedom from these traps.

When I see a potential client walk through my doors and he isn't willing to recognize his role in the fight, I know we are in trouble. If someone is in denial, how can we win?

Many people are not capable of managing conflict because they are in denial and never acknowledge they have these struggles in their lives. The first order of business to win over struggles is to acknowledge they are present. Once a person admits he struggles with food or alcohol, he can start healing and conquering. Many times it is easier to live in denial than defeat a deep-rooted trap. A lot of people say I will quit drinking next week; or, I only drink on weekends; or, I will start a health plan after I eat this chocolate chip cookie, when they fully know they do not tend to do anything about it.

I quit drinking alcohol twenty-four years ago. It was hard. I took advantage of several tools, such as AA, counseling, and group therapy, to beat the alcohol trap. I enjoyed the journey, but I had to change people, places, and things. For me to win, I had to move to another town. I had to learn to manage not only the daily struggles but the weekend struggles as well. I caught myself early on the progressive disease graph, but I fully acknowledged that I abused alcohol. I thank God for the strength to maintain my sobriety and learn to live one day at a time.

The most interesting tool that I implemented to really re-move myself from the alcoholism trap was journaling. I had to learn to manage my feelings, and I used this tool to teach me to develop ten action items daily that helped me manage my feelings. After a period of time, I learned that the action items that helped me manage my feelings were always the same. I needed to live one day at a time. I needed to pray and trust God. I needed to work out daily as well as trust God. Most importantly, I learned that I needed to have fun. What a blessing!

How about you? No matter what your conflict or struggle is, you gotta PUSH!

EXERCISE
Things Left

Write about one person in your life for whom you have things in your heart that are left unsaid. This person can be a family member, friend, coworker, church member, etc. What is it that you need to tell this person? It may be as simple as "I love you!" It may be as difficult as you need to let them go. This is a time to free your heart of anything that is holding you back and keeping you from your freedom. YOU have to PUSH! into this exercise to really get the most out of it. Make a mature plan to resolve any remaining issues.

_____

_____

_____

_____

_____

_____

EXERCISE

Success

Write ten things that you do that keep you from being successful.

_____   _____

_____   _____

_____   _____

_____   _____

_____   _____

Write ten things you need to do to convert the barriers into building blocks of success.

_____   _____

_____   _____

_____   _____

_____   _____

_____   _____

Key Takeaways

- Never, ever give up.

- Attitude is everything.

- If you can't get a miracle, be one.

- Winners are persistent.

- Dream big.

- No matter who you are and how successful you may be, you need to be free.

- People deserve a second chance.

- You cannot change or heal what you do not acknowledge.

- God's grace is about taking the absolute worst day of your life and making it the absolute best.

- People who experience fear of failure usually lean toward perfection.

- People who have fear of success are usually the ones who set themselves up to fail.

- Successful people live outside the box.

- Anger directed at someone else is the poison that kills you.

- Take care of yourself so you can take care of others.

- No matter how hard it gets, put your armor on every morning and go to work.

- We cannot condemn our kids for making bad choices if we haven't prepared them to make good ones.

- God doesn't want us to feel the spirit of fear, but He wants us to feel power, love, and sound mind.

- If you want to get somewhere in life, you better start learning about other people and their wants.

- Guard your heart.

PUSH!

ABOUT THE AUTHOR

Brett Stalcup graduated cum laude from Texas Tech University with a degree in finance. He graduated from Texas Tech University School of Law in 1984. He began his law career working for the legendary Dallas County District Attorney Henry Wade.

In 1989 he went into private practice as a criminal defense lawyer. He was recognized as a leading criminal defense lawyer in 1990 after successfully litigating high-profile cases such as the murder case against Dana McIntosh. He was one of the founding attorneys who developed a recovery defense strategy for drug- and alcohol-related offenses.

Many of his recovery defense cases involve juvenile and young adult offenders. These cases often involve parents who are stressed to the point of divorce. Brett offers his clients more than legal advice; he offers them counseling by sharing his life experience and wisdom.

Over time, as wayward youth replaced their self-destructive habits with success-oriented life skills and families were reconciled, Brett defined a vision for a new organization. He founded Discovery Training, a life skills organization. In 2008 he was recognized as a leading family law attorney and coach.

While at Discovery Training, Brett authored numerous articles, syllabi, and life skills workshop programs. He gave counseling to individuals, couples, and entire families. He gave motivational presentations and life skills training to large audiences at Discovery Training seminars.

During this time, he also practiced business law. He has

successfully litigated complex business, condemnation, and oil and gas cases. In one condemnation case, the client was awarded $1.65 million, which was two times the original Texas Department of Transportation offer.

Brett balances his professional life with a rich and rewarding personal life. He is married and has two children. He is a consultant to La Hacienda, a drug and alcohol treatment program, and is a past consultant to their outpatient program director. He is an advocate for the homeless and volunteers at Austin Street Centre. He has a black belt in aikido.

Information about Brett Stalcup's practice of law can be found at www.stalcuplaw.com. Brett's schedule of appearances is published on the PUSH! Program web site at www. PushProgram.com.

Your job is to take the worst thing that happens to you and turn it into the best—to PUSH!

Journal Pages

Journal Pages

Journal Pages

Journal Pages

Journal Pages

Journal Pages

Journal Pages

Journal Pages

Journal Pages

Journal Pages

Journal Pages

Journal Pages

Journal Pages

_____

_____

_____

_____

_____

_____

_____

_____

_____

_____

_____

_____

_____

_____

_____

_____

_____

_____

_____

_____

_____

Journal Pages

Journal Pages

Journal Pages

Journal Pages

Journal Pages

Journal Pages

Journal Pages